JIM WHITEWOLF

HAPPY BIRTHDAY TO J BRACKEN
FROM JIM 11 OCTOBER 1977

JIM WHITEWOLF

The Life of a
Kiowa Apache Indian

*Edited and with an
Introduction and Epilogue
by*
Charles S. Brant
University of Alberta

Dover Publications, Inc.
New York

Published in Canada by General Publishing Company, Ltd.,
30 Lesmill Road, Don Mills, Toronto, Ontario
Published in the United Kingdom by Constable and Company, Ltd.,
10 Orange Street, London, W.C.2

Jim Whitewolf: The Life of a Kiowa Apache Indian
is a new work, published for the first time by
Dover Publications, Inc., in 1969

Standard Book Number: 486-22015-X
Library of Congress Catalog Card Number: 67-25596

Manufactured in the United States of America
Dover Publications, Inc.
180 Varick Street, New York, N.Y. 10014

For Eric, Roger
and Jane

Preface

ALTHOUGH for humanists in the wider sense autobiography has long held an established place as a literary form in Western European culture, only infrequently have life histories portrayed individuals in non-Western and especially non-literate traditions. Cultural anthropologists, on the other hand, have discovered during the past few decades that autobiographies, as told by native subjects and meticulously recorded by the ethnographer, can provide varied, added dimensions of insight into the working of a culture and social system as well as of personality-in-culture. Such insights may not be obtainable from a study of the muted descriptive discourse of an ethnological monograph. With particular reference to the North American Indian field, one needs only to recall the light shed by Paul Radin's pioneering book *Crashing Thunder* (1926) on Winnebago culture, Walter Dyk's *Son of Old Man Hat* (1938) on Navaho, or Leo Simmons's *Sun Chief* (1942) on the Hopi.[1] It is hoped that *Jim Whitewolf: The Life of a Kiowa Apache Indian* will represent a useful addition to this kind of anthropological literature.

In what follows I have tried to present a life history which will convey some feeling for the reality of a man's experiences under conditions of stressful culture contact and social disorganization. Here will be found the autobiography neither of chief nor of priest, neither of warrior nor of peacemaker: Jim Whitewolf was in most respects an ordinary member of his tribe. Born at a time when the foundations of his native culture were undermined by the incursions of the white man into tribal territory—his people confined to the limits of a reservation and his native religion scorned and condemned by zealous Christian missionaries—he lived through more than seventy years of radical social transformations. The cultural and historical background of his life experiences has been sketched in the Introduction. Mirrored in Jim's story are tribal and individual reactions to the assorted virtues and vices brought to the Kiowa Apache by Euro-American civilization, such as individualism in

[1] See also Radin's *The Autobiography of a Winnebago Indian*. University of California Press, 1920 (New York: Dover Publications, Inc., 1963).

property, Christianity, modern education and alcohol. Here, then, are the achievements and failures, the hopes, fears and disappointments experienced by one tribesman through some three-quarters of a century spanning a critical phase of his people's history.

The material in these pages was gathered by me during the late winter of 1948 and early spring of 1949 as it was told to me by Jim Whitewolf. Our daily sessions of several hours each occupied a period of about five weeks. Although he spoke moderately fluent English, Jim felt from the outset that he could present some aspects of his story better in his own language. I therefore secured the services of Wallace Whitebone, a nephew of Jim. On a few occasions when interpreter and informant could not be brought together conveniently, and at all times that Jim felt he could communicate adequately in English, I recorded parts of the narrative directly from him. Jim tended strongly to think and speak in terms of the qualities of actions and events much more than in temporal terms; this habit may well be due to the influence of his native language, which stresses aspects and qualities and does not pay the attention to time and chronology that English does. To introduce some semblance of chronology into the life history I have made certain rearrangements of the material. Here and there grammatical changes were required to eliminate ambiguities. Explanatory footnotes have been provided on points which might not otherwise be clear to some readers. In all other respects, the story stands as it was told.

In order to protect the privacy of all individuals involved, names of all major figures in Jim's narrative, including Jim's own, have been fictionalized.

In bringing this work to completion my obligations are several. Jim Whitewolf displayed patience and forbearance in unfolding to me, always an outsider and at first a stranger, the intimate as well as the mundane aspects of his life; he did so with full knowledge and willingness that eventually the story would be published. Had he lived to see this, I am sure he would have been proud to be the subject of a book. Wallace Whitebone, my interpreter, spent many hours patiently translating portions of Jim's account into English. To the Wenner-Gren Foundation for Anthropological Research (then the Viking Fund) I am grateful for their grant of a fellowship which made possible the research project of which this book is one product. Professor Morris Edward Opler of Cornell University initially suggested the project and throughout the course of my field work and subsequent analysis of the material provided generously of his deep and rich knowledge of Apache Indian cultures. I owe thanks to Professor William E. Bittle and to Judy Jordan, University of Oklahoma, for obtaining data on Jim's life pertaining to the period subsequent to my field work. Valerie Czajkowski and Victoria Bobowski, formerly secretaries in the Department of Sociology and Anthropology, University of Alberta, patiently and expertly typed the manuscript.

Charles S. Brant

Edmonton, Alberta, Canada
February, 1968

Contents

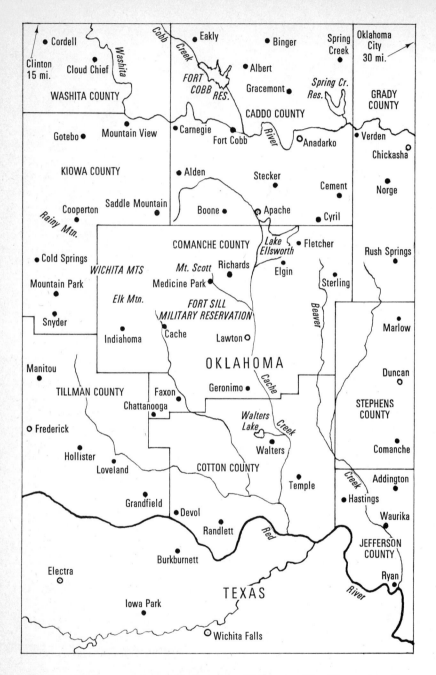

Sections of nine counties of southwestern Oklahoma. The Kiowa Apache
live near the towns of Fort Cobb and Apache.

Introduction

The Cultural and Historical Background

THE KIOWA APACHE, presently living on government allotments of land near the towns of Fort Cobb and Apache in southwestern Oklahoma, are an Apachean-speaking people who, in pre-contact times, ranged both further north and south, at times reaching Mexico on raids for horses and captives. Never numbering more than about three hundred fifty, they have been traditionally associated with the much larger Kiowa tribe, a people speaking an entirely unrelated language and following a mode of life typical of Indians of the Great Plains area. So far as Kiowa Apache tradition goes, they have never known a time when they were not associated with the Kiowa. This, however, does not mean that the Kiowa Apache were in any sense merely a segment of the Kiowa; they were a distinct cultural entity, but roved the Plains region in close proximity to the Kiowa, probably for reasons of security from dangers posed by much larger, warlike peoples. On such major ceremonial occasions as the Sun Dance, they camped with the Kiowa and functioned as a band in the camp circle. They had their own leaders in the hunt and in warfare and their own distinctive body of custom and traditions. Contrary to the premature conclusion voiced by certain writers that the Kiowa Apache were very similar culturally to the Kiowa, closer investigation reveals important differences in social organization, folklore and beliefs. A large number of these features, when cast in comparative ethnological perspective, show unmistakably that the nearest cultural relatives of the Kiowa Apache are the eastern groups of Apache of New Mexico, especially the Jicarilla and Lipan Apache. Likewise, many of the Plains features in Kiowa Apache culture, by their very weakness and vagueness, such as the dancing societies and shield groups, reflect the relative recency of Plains cultural influence and lack of deep integration of Plains patterns in Kiowa Apache

I

culture.[1] The presumption is strong that about 250 to 300 years ago the Kiowa Apache were a small group fronting the Western Plains and were pushed, by the incursions of larger, more powerful tribes, onto the Plains proper, where they subsequently joined the Kiowa. From that time on, historical evidence points to much movement in the Plains in the company of the Kiowa, as far north as the Black Hills region, and after 1780, a steady southward movement to their present location.

1

IN ECONOMY and material aspects of their culture the Kiowa Apache adapted themselves to Plains life, hunting the buffalo and making their tools, clothing and shelter from its various parts. Other animals of considerable importance in their lives were the elk, antelope and deer. Leggings, moccasins and jackets were made of buckskin, as were women's dresses. Containers of various sorts were carved of wood, there being no tradition of basketry or pottery; and water was transported in bags made from the paunch of the buffalo. Horn served for spoons, while knives were made of flint, later of metal when contact began with the white man. The horse was the means of transportation for these people, often dragging behind it the travois of poles on which various goods were carried. Prior to the acquisition of horses, a period of which there is but the faintest and most legendary recollection, the dog was the Kiowa Apache beast of burden. In addition to their game animals, which provided the basis of the diet, the Kiowa Apache collected a wide variety of wild fruits, nuts and roots which served as foodstuffs as well as for the preparation of native medicines.

Traditions speak of considerable nomadism and of raid and warfare with many groups—the Ute to the west, the Pawnee, Sioux and the Mexicans to the south. Doubtless the Kiowa Apache often

---

[1] These points have been elaborated in my articles "The Cultural Position of the Kiowa Apache," in *Southwestern Journal of Anthropology*, 5 : 1 (1949), 56–61, and "Kiowa Apache Culture History: Some Further Observations," in *Southwestern Journal of Anthropology*, 9 : 2 (1953), 195–202. See also my "The Kiowa Apache Indians: A Study in Ethnology and Acculturation" (unpublished Ph.D. dissertation, Cornell University, 1951).

accompanied the Kiowa on long raids southward for horses and prisoners, raids which gave cause for anxiety to the government even after initial treaties were signed and settlement on reservations had begun.

In their social system, the Kiowa Apache lived in a tightly knit group, small in numbers, in which every person was related in one way or another to every other person. All of one's cousins were his "brothers" and "sisters"; grandparent's siblings were grandparents as much as were actual grandparents. The term for "father" was extended to father's brother and mother's sister's husband; that for "mother" to mother's sister and father's brother's wife. Kinship was all-important and the extended domestic family, embracing several generations, was the hub of the system. Deference and respect was paid to the aged, age being a criterion of experience and wisdom. The family was the unit of economic cooperation, being augmented and strengthened by the support of sons-in-law married into it. The Kiowa Apache had a slight preference for matrilocal residence, the expectation being that a daughter's husband would live at her family camp at least initially, perhaps moving off with the girl at a later time to set up a separate household. Polygyny was known and practiced in former times, although the wealth required in the exchange of gifts at marriage probably made monogamy the practice for most of the tribe. Upon the death of his wife, a man was obligated, unless released by his spouse's family, to marry an eligible sister; conversely, a woman was expected to marry a brother of her deceased husband. Thus, the cultural expectations revolving around the marriage tie, creating various rights and duties, bound families together in a close and intimate manner.

There seems to have been no fixed hereditary succession to chieftainship, nor was the office elective. In a tribe so small in numbers, men of outstanding ability were readily known, and chieftainship seems to have been a highly informal matter, both in selection and in the execution of the office. Age and proven ability in the hunt and raid were the normal criteria of leadership.

All indications suggest that problems of maintenance of social order were minimal. Aboriginal patterns of sharing and mutual aid extended to the use of tools and food, and apparently intra-tribal theft was virtually unknown. Disputes of various kinds, often over women, did occasionally arise, but an effort was always made to settle these amicably. The role of mediator fell to the chief. In the event of a killing, the immediate family of the guilty person was expected to make a payment, normally in the form of horses, to the family of the deceased. The chief had the responsibility of interceding whenever attempts at direct retaliation were imminent.

Kiowa Apache religion was concerned mainly with individual utilization of supernatural power, which one might acquire from animals, plants or forces of nature such as lightning and thunder. The method of obtaining supernatural power might consist in an active quest for a vision, but often it involved no positive action at all; rather, power came to the person during a dream or other passive state. It appears that the active vision quest, in the common Plains pattern—self-isolation, fasting and thirsting, smoking and praying in an abject, humble manner—was the far less commonly practiced mode of securing power.

Supernatural power was conceived of as being intrinsically neutral in its nature; whether it was used for good or for evil purposes was determined by its possessor and his character. Thus it presented a dual aspect to the Kiowa Apache and it is not surprising that their attitudes toward power and those who wielded it were quite ambivalent. Thus an informant said, "J had a lot of power, they say. He could pray for someone and the person would get well. But I heard that medicine men could do you harm. One of them might see a nice-looking girl somewhere and ask for her. If they wouldn't give her to him he might make them or her sick." Individuals are known to have received power, only to refuse to accept it, out of uncertainty and fear.

Despite its fearsome aspect and potential dangers to the user, power was accepted by many Kiowa Apache and became the means to considerable prestige and income. Shamans noted for their curative abilities, their skill in clairvoyant forecasting of events or their feats of legerdemain, enjoyed the acclaim and patronage of their fellow tribesmen.

If the shaman failed to bring about the patient's recovery, he informed him that his power was weak and that he should seek another shaman's aid. The gifts which had been proferred were then returned to the patient or to his primary kin. The shaman who began to lose cases suspected the possibility that he had broken some rule imparted to him by his power at the time he had received it and thus had incurred the power's anger. To others, the unsuccessful shaman sometimes appeared as a mere pretender. If his patients were dying in numbers he was likely to be regarded as a witch.

No discussion of Kiowa Apache religion would be adequate without mention of witchcraft, a phenomenon closely associated with the securing and utilization of supernatural power. It was, indeed, the neutral character of power itself, implying the possibility of its use for evil, that made for the distrustful attitude and ambivalent feelings toward those who had traffic with the supernatural. An informant related this story:

> When I was young I was inquisitive. My grandmother had some kind of medicine, so I asked her once, "Are you a doctor?"
> She said, "Sure I am."
> I asked, "Do you witch?" She just laughed. She said she had medicine to cure with. I was kind of scared.

It was believed that repeated fainting spells were indicative that a person was suffering from witchcraft. Any sickness which persisted and did not yield to the efforts of numerous shamans was very likely to be proclaimed the result of a witch's work. The implication that shamans practiced extortion by the use of their powers for evil purposes is a note frequently sounded by Kiowa Apaches in talking about the supernatural. Apparently, in aboriginal times there were individuals who amassed considerable wealth by such means and were generally feared throughout the tribe. A few informants spoke of the killing of witches in the old days but none was able to furnish actual instances. One stated that "usually you hired the shaman who diagnosed the witching to witch back for you."

Aboriginal Kiowa Apache religion was composed of more, however, than the individual quest for supernatural power, or the visitation of powers to the person, with the utilization of such power in curing and sorcery. There was a rather vague, generalized conception of a deity which the Kiowa Apache called *nuakolahe*, literally, "earth he made it." To him was attributed the creation of the earth, its geographic features and its human, plant and animal inhabitants. This deity was considered responsible for creating the tribal culture heroes, Fireboy and Waterboy, the twins who are portrayed in Kiowa Apache mythology. Through a series of exploits these culture heroes slew the enemies of mankind and made the earth safe for the people. Concerning the Creator, an informant said, "He started everything in the world; everything belongs to him. When you prayed, you prayed first to him."

Dimly remembered today are the Kiowa Apache medicine bundles and their functions. Four in number, these fetish objects were tribal property, passed down in certain family lines, in which their custody was entrusted. They were small bundles covered with cloth or leather on the outside. Inside were small bits of cloth, leather and other objects. In the case of two of these bundles, according to informants, there were pictographic representations of their myths of origin. Annually, the bundles were opened, each having a particular ceremony that was performed at a certain time of the year. At other times, an individual could go to the keeper of a bundle and address prayers to it.

These sacred fetishes, often referred to by the Kiowa Apache as "worships," were regarded with awe and reverence. There were many taboos associated with them. For example, one could not whistle near a bundle or play a gambling game in its immediate vicinity.

Concerning the prayers addressed to the bundles, an informant stated:

> You would pray to a bundle if there was something you wanted. You took a piece of cloth and covered the bundle as you prayed. You didn't really pray to the bundle but to the power. In the old days they used to pray to these bundles' powers before they went on the warpath, so they would return safely. The water-medicine bundle ceremony could be put on whenever someone who had a sick relative wanted it put on for that person.

The informant concluded his account of the medicine bundles with the following words, which are indicative of the attitudes toward these fetishes:

> I don't talk to you about the medicine bundles in the same way that I tell you the coyote stories. I have a different feeling inside. I believe in them.[2]

[2] This explicit differentiation by the informant between his feelings toward the sacred and secular aspects of his culture is interesting. The coyote stories consist of a cycle of traditional tales concerning the trickster figure Coyote, semi-human, semi-animal, who epitomizes all that is foolish, selfish and reprehensible in the Kiowa Apache world view. Quite frequently the stories have a bawdy aspect, and in the informal gatherings in which they were related, the audience, composed of both sexes, young and old, responded with loud guffaws of laughter to the recounting of Coyote's misdeeds.

Ceremonials among the Kiowa Apache were carried on by four dance societies. These societies were very roughly age-graded: the *Kasowe* or Rabbit Society was for the young, from small toddlers up to the age of about twelve to fifteen years; the *Manitidie* and *Klintidie* were adult male groups; the *Izuwe* was an old women's group. There was, however, no rigidly fixed sequence through which an individual passed. While it was rare for a child not to participate in the Rabbit Society at some time, he might very well never go on to membership in the adult societies. As a matter of fact, informants frequently reported that adult men evaded becoming members of the *Manitidie* and *Klintidie*, disliking the obligations they involved, and, in the case of the *Klintidie*, fearing the risks of life and limb expected of one.

Kasowe (*Rabbit*) *Society*[3]

Practically every child belonged to the *Kasowe* or Rabbit Society. As soon as a child was old enough to take part in the dancing, he joined this group. The meetings required the presence of the custodian of one of the medicine bundles, which was associated with the Rabbit Society. These meetings were sponsored by particular families on the occasion of a child's illness, or for the purpose of aiding his future well-being.

An essential part of the meeting consisted of prayers uttered by the bundle custodian for the health and long life of the child for whom the meeting was called. The meeting was then given over to dancing in which the children hopped up and down in imitation of rabbits. Their participation in the dancing was enforced by the "bull," an older boy who carried a whip and a knife and who might strike a child or cut his hair for failure to cooperate. The singing that accompanied the Rabbit Society dancing contained a certain amount of obscene reference to the rabbit's anatomy and behavior, which evoked much laughter from those present. After the dance, food was brought in and a contest took place between groups seated on opposite sides of the tipi to see which group could consume more.

[3] The material that follows on Kiowa Apache ceremonial organization is based largely upon McAllister's account. Cf. J. Gilbert McAllister, "Kiowa-Apache Social Organization," in F. Eggan (ed.), *Social Anthropology of North American Tribes* (Chicago, 1937), pp. 139–42, 150–57.

This society provided an opportunity for Kiowa Apache young-sters to become acquainted from an early age and to form bonds of friendship that often endured throughout their lives.

Manitidie (Adult Male) Society

This was a dance for adult males which was concerned with war-fare and raiding. The members were paired, each one having a partner with whom he sat and danced at the meetings of the group. Partners cooperated in raiding and fighting, painting themselves alike. In many respects this was a form of ritual kinship.

The *Manitidie* officers included four chiefs, two *bacaye*, who led in capturing new members for the group, and a "bull" who super-vised the dances. Meetings usually took place before war and raid parties set out on their missions. There was an annual spring dance of the *Manitidie* at which the four ceremonial staffs were rewrapped with otterskin and buck sinew. These staffs were always handed down to men considered brave and worthy. Usually they remained in given families and were passed down in the male line.

An important function of the *Manitidie* society was policing. When the Kiowa Apache camp moved, the *Manitidie* were charged with keeping order in the ranks. The same police function was car-ried on during communal hunts of larger game. The *Manitidie* had power to whip a recalcitrant individual, kill his horse or take his property. Occasionally the *Manitidie* engaged in contests among themselves, or in informal groups challenged members of the *Klintidie*, the other adult male society of the Kiowa Apache. All of these activities are Plains-like in orientation. However, it is important to note that "there were no organized contests nor any antagonism between these two groups, nor any privileged license with the wives of the other group as is sometimes found on the Plains."[4]

Klintidie (Adult Male) Society

This was a much smaller group of men, the oldest and bravest of the tribe. As in the *Manitidie*, members were paired in the fashion of "blood brothers." Although wives did not belong to the group, they could attend its meetings.

[4] McAllister, *op. cit.*, p. 153.

The meetings were held at irregular intervals, which members could not fail to attend, on pain of being taunted in public with the remark: "You are going to marry your mother-in-law."[5]

In this group, the members were noted for "talking backward." Commands and orders meant exactly their opposite; in battle an order to retreat meant to attack, and vice versa. Indeed, the *Klintidie* were distinguished for their extreme bravery in combat:

> They would ride up to the thickest of the fight and jump off their pony, slapping it to make it run away. Those wearing the trailing bands would "plant" themselves at a dangerous spot by sticking an arrow through the end of the band. Only another person could release them by pulling out the arrow and telling them to "stay there."[6]

The *Klintidie* society had an unusual feature in its connection with the owl, one of the most feared and mysterious animals known to the Kiowa Apache. Owl feathers were used in the headdress and sometimes worn on the shoulders by *Klintidie* members. If an owl hooted or someone mimicked the owl's cry during battle, the *Klintidie* had to stand their ground, no matter what the situation was. In ceremony such a cry required that the dancing go on, even though the group might have danced through an entire night. One of the leaders was called "Owl Man" or "Ghost Man." His behavior at meetings was strongly sexual:

> Sometimes during large gatherings he would completely disrobe; he might even have sexual intercourse with a woman publicly. He was privileged to cohabit with any woman who did not keep away from him. But if a woman could not avoid him, she could protect herself by saying, "Do it to me," and then he could not touch her. After a public exhibition of this sort, he would carefully dress himself and then pray for the health and happiness of all. During the meetings of the *Klintidie* this man might arise, remove his loin cloth, pull up his

---

[5] Among the Kiowa Apache, as with all other Apachean peoples except the Lipan, mother-in-law avoidance was strictly observed by men. A Kiowa Apache man would not even look at his mother-in-law, much less have any physical contact with her.

[6] McAllister, *op. cit.*, pp. 154–55. Cf. Alice Marriott, *The Ten Grandmothers* (Norman, University of Oklahoma Press, 1944), p. 33, for an account of similar behavior in the Kiowa "Crazy Dog" Society.

blanket, and back up to each member, exposing his private parts. Women were present.[7]

Izuwe (Old Women's) Society

Almost nothing is known of this organization. It died out long ago, and it was, moreover, a secret society. Its meetings were held at the sponsorship of a man who had asked for the Izuwe's prayers for success at the time of going on a raid and had returned. The women would ritually smoke a pipe which he prepared and held in turn to the mouth of each member. When raiding parties returned, the Izuwe held a dance. One old man, who served as drummer, was the sole male participant in the Izuwe. The tipi in which the dances were held was partitioned so that no outsiders could look through the door and observe the activities. During the Kiowa Apache scalp dance, the Izuwe would bite the scalps, wrists, ears or other anatomical trophies the men had brought back as evidence of victory.

IN THE foregoing pages we have briefly outlined features of Kiowa Apache society and culture which prevailed in aboriginal times. Although in a state of disintegration by the time of Jim Whitewolf's birth, they nevertheless provide a meaningful setting for understanding much in his life story. It is equally valuable, for this purpose, to have some knowledge of the continuing process of change during his lifetime, and of the sociocultural conditions which prevailed during the latter years of his life.[8]

2

FOR the earlier part of this contact continuum and acculturation process we must depend on such diverse and scattered sources as the reports of explorers and travellers and the accounts by the

---

[7] McAllister, op. cit., p. 155.

[8] The material following, which concerns white contact and its impact on Kiowa Apache society, has also appeared in my article "White Contact and Cultural Disintegration Among the Kiowa Apache," *Plains Anthropologist*, 9 : 23 (1964). The account of the modern community is drawn from my "The Kiowa Apache Indians: A Study in Ethnology and Acculturation" (Ph. D. dissertation, Cornell University, 1951).

government officials assigned to the area. We shall not, therefore, be able to present the fully detailed description and analysis that would be possible if we had several fully rounded accounts of the culture based on observations made at intervals over the total time span. Nonetheless, even from the relatively sparse material at hand, the general outlines of the acculturation process emerge and the contemporary situation becomes illuminated by. a knowledge of the major events of the past.

The first treaty involving the Kiowa Apache was signed in 1837; it was also signed by the Kiowa and Tawakoni Indians. The terms of this treaty included

> peace and friendship, with forgiveness of past injuries, and satisfactory settlement of future disputes that might arise between these western tribes and the Osage, Muscogee (Creek), and citizens of the United States. All the tribes concerned were to have equal hunting rights on the southern prairies as far west as the jurisdiction of the government extended, and citizens of the United States were to have free right of travel to and from Mexico and Texas through the Indian hunting grounds.[9]

This treaty was followed with respect to peace with the Osage and Creeks and also with regard to the rights of United States citizens, with one exception. After the annexation of Texas by the United States in 1845, depredations by the Indians took place, for they still regarded Texans as foreigners who hitherto had driven them out of old hunting grounds.[10]

From this time until 1865, according to Mooney, the history of the Kiowa Apache was "that of the Kiowa." This would indicate that they were frequently engaged in raiding southward into Texas and Mexico for horses and captives. With the Kiowa they must have suffered to some extent from the smallpox epidemic of 1839–40 and the cholera epidemic ten years later. In 1853, together with the Kiowa and Comanche, the Kiowa Apache signed another treaty with the government, whereby they agreed to remain at peace with both the United States and Mexico and gave the United States government the right to establish roads and military posts in their

---

[9] James Mooney, *Calendar History of the Kiowa Indians*, Seventeenth Annual Report of the Bureau of American Ethnology (Washington: U.S. Government Printing Office, 1898), p. 169.

[10] *Ibid.*

territory. An annuity of eighteen thousand dollars was granted these tribes for ten years, with provision for extension of another five years.

In the following year, 1854, the Kiowa Apache, in alliance with the Comanche, Kiowa and Cheyenne, made war against tribes living in eastern Kansas. The motivation was apparently due to the pressures of a decreasing supply of bison. Despite the fact that these allied tribes had an advantage in manpower of fifteen to one over their Sauk and Fox adversaries, they were very badly defeated because the latter possessed rifles.[11]

Intermittent raiding and warfare continued until the Treaty of the Little Arkansas in 1865. This agreement actually consisted of three concordats between the government and various Indian tribes. On October 17, 1865, the Kiowa Apache agreed to a treaty which provided that they be detached from the Kiowa and Comanche and attached to the Cheyenne and Arapaho. The latter tribes relinquished their reservation in southeastern Colorado and took up land in Kansas and Indian Territory.[12]

By 1867 the federal government had determined to stop the raiding and warfare in the Plains area that was interfering with the development of the railroads and white settlement. A commission appointed by Congress met the Cheyenne, Arapaho, Kiowa, Comanche and Kiowa Apache on Medicine Lodge Creek, near the present site of Medicine Lodge, Kansas. The Kiowa Apache, at their own request, were reunited to the Kiowa and Comanche. The treaty provided for a reservation for these three tribes, "bounded on the east by the ninety-eighth meridian, on the south and west by Red river and its North-fork, and on the north by the Washita from the ninety-eighth meridian up to a point 30 miles by river from Fort Cobb, and thence by a line due west to the North fork."[13] Provision was made for schools, an agency, a doctor and a blacksmith. All previous treaty obligations of the United States were canceled by this treaty,

and instead the government agrees to deliver at the agency "on the 15th day of October each year, for thirty years," the equivalent of a full suit of clothing for each Indian man, woman, and child, for which

[11] *Ibid.*, p. 174.

[12] *Annual Report of the Commissioner of Indian Affairs to the Secretary of the Interior for 1865* (Washington: U.S. Government Printing Office), pp. 47, 527. Mooney, *op. cit.*, p. 180.

[13] Mooney, *op. cit.*, pp. 184–85.

purpose the agent is to make an annual census of the tribes; "and in addition to the clothing herein named, the sum of twenty-five thousand dollars shall be annually appropriated for a period of thirty years" for the judicious purchase of such articles as may seem proper to the condition and necessities of the Indians.[14]

So the scene was set for a period which was to see, within three decades, the breakdown of the aboriginal way of life and the disorganization of Kiowa Apache society. This was a period in which the government attempted to change a nomadic, hunting, warring group into a settled, agricultural, peaceful people. We shall presently see the outcome of these efforts.

From the start of this period it is interesting to note that the Kiowa Apache were spoken of as more cooperative and obedient than the other tribes within the reservation's jurisdiction. In the Annual Report for 1872, the tribes of the reservation were generally characterized as "wild and intractable"; they showed "no signs of improvement"; and they carried out very little cultivation of the land. The Kiowa Apache, however, were noted later in the same report as "better disposed than their associates . . . if they can be removed from the evil influences of the Kiowas and Comanches they will do well."[15] In 1873, "The Apaches were very attentive, working themselves with the hoe." And again, they "have remained quiet; they seem very anxious to settle down and become farmers."[16] Throughout the 1870's the same note of optimism was sounded by a succession of agents in references to the Kiowa Apache under their jurisdiction, in contrast to the Kiowa and Comanche, who were still inclined to engage in raiding and warfare.

In the next decade, however, things took a turn for the worse, owing, according to Agency reports, to the rapidly decreasing supply of bison and other game animals on the reservation and the consequent pressure of an insufficient food supply. We learn from the report for 1882 that there was considerable butchering of allotted cattle herds by the Indians. This was related to the fact that the original government food ration was computed on the basis of

[14] *Ibid.*
[15] *Annual Report of the Commissioner of Indian Affairs to the Secretary of the Interior for 1872* (Washington: U.S. Government Printing Office), pp. 41, 138.
[16] *Annual Report of the Commissioner of Indian Affairs to the Secretary of the Interior for 1873* (Washington: U.S. Government Printing Office), p. 219.

the difference between total food needs and the amount of food the Indians could supply for themselves by hunting, but no upward revision of the ration had been made despite the rapid decrease in game animals.[17] The agent complained of considerable gambling by the Indians and the selling of horses in order to obtain money with which to gamble. Also, a lively trade in whisky from Texas was taking place. In 1886 the Kiowa Apache were reported to be stealing ponies and cattle from the Caddo and Comanche and using them for food because of the poor quality of the government cattle issue.

Throughout this period of stress the power of chiefs and shamans was declining, the extended family units were breaking down into smaller conjugal groups, the old religion was fading. We learn of the beginning of the use of peyote, obtained from Indians in the south. The missionaries began to appear in the area in numbers, erecting schools and churches and beginning their efforts to convert the Kiowa Apache to Christianity.

In 1892 the Kiowa Apache were struck by an epidemic of whooping cough, measles and pneumonia, which killed many infants and children. The population in 1891 of 325 declined in one year to 241. In 1892 a delegation of Indians went to Washington to request permission to lease reservation grazing lands to outsiders, a matter looked upon negatively by the Indians a decade earlier.[18] The right of leasing was granted by the government and there was "great joy" at the news.

Our knowledge of this critical period in Kiowa Apache history is interrupted by the absence of a report for the jurisdiction in the two succeeding years, 1893 and 1894. We may be sure, however, that the general situation became worse, with resulting chaos in the administration of the Agency, for in 1895 we are told in the report of Frank D. Baldwin, Temporary Civilian Agent, how at the time he took office he found the Agency and its records disorganized. The equipment issued to the Indians for farming purposes was rusting and rotting in the brush and a general condition of demoralization prevailed. Some of the Agency records were even found in the

[17] *Annual Report of the Commissioner of Indian Affairs to the Secretary of the Interior for 1882* (Washington: U.S. Government Printing Office), p. 64.

[18] *Annual Report of the Commissioner of Indian Affairs to the Secretary of the Interior for 1892* (Washington: U.S. Government Printing Office), p. 387. Cf. *Annual Report for 1883*, pp. 71–72.

Agency lavatory being used as toilet paper! With reference to the Kiowa Apache the agent wrote:

> I find the Apaches the most indolent and shiftless and poorest of all the tribes on the reservation. They won't work unless forced to, and with very few exceptions are a people that we can have little hope for.[19]

In the following year the Indians were reported to be very uneasy about the treaty of September, 1892, providing for the opening of their reservation to white settlement. Some denied ever signing it. The agent was of the opinion that force was used to obtain some of the signatures.[20] In the same report the agent voiced the opinion that the Indians were in no condition to become self-supporting. Alluding to the aboriginal nomadic habits of these people, he warned of the dangers in the opening of the reservation to white settlers before the end of an additional five-year period.[21]

But warnings were of no avail. The westward movement of white settlers in search of homesteads and the determination of the government to "civilize" the Indian in the white American image by making him an owner of individual property converged to result in individual allotment of the reservation, beginning in 1901. With great foresight the Indian Agent wrote in his report for 1900:

> It is thought that much disappointment will be experienced by those who will locate on the lands made surplus after the Indians are served with their allotments, with expectation of profitably farming the same. This reasoning is based upon the fact that the Indians are given their choice of the best lands which are reasonably well adapted to agriculture, which is assurance that after the authorized deductions are made for school lands, etc., there will be but a limited number of

[19] *Annual Report of the Commissioner of Indian Affairs to the Secretary of the Interior for 1895* (Washington: U.S. Government Printing Office), p. 250.

[20] This treaty, known as the Jerome Treaty, resulted in the sale of a large portion of the reservation. In March and April, 1949, while in the field, the writer learned that the Indian Claims Commission was then considering the claims of the Kiowa, Kiowa Apache and Comanche tribes against the government growing out of alleged violation of the treaty terms. The Indians asserted that they received only about one-half of the price per acre stipulated in the treaty. The total claim was about sixteen million dollars.

[21] *Annual Report of the Commissioner of Indian Affairs to the Secretary of the Interior* (Washington: U.S. Government Printing Office, 1896), pp. 255–56.

desirable quarter sections left for actual settlers to locate as home-steads.

This resolves into the prospect for the future that a majority of successful white inhabitants of this reservation will be renters of Indian lands, and that unless stringent rules are adopted respecting the character of the renters permitted to enter into contract with the Indians, their progress in civilization and self-support will be slow at best, if not actually retarded by the association.[22]

The forecast that many white farmers would become renters of Indian lands was only too correct. These and other leasing arrangements were to have far-reaching consequences for the course of Indian culture, as we shall see presently.

From 1901 to 1903 the process of individual allotment of reservation lands took place. Each member of the Kiowa Apache tribe, regardless of age, received an allotment of 160 acres during this period. In 1908 a subsequent allotment was made to take care of persons born between 1903 and 1908. This disposed of surplus land.

The Kiowa Apache allotments numbered one hundred fifty in all, scattered over twenty-one townships in southwestern Oklahoma, ranging from the Washita River southward to the Red River. Title to these lands resided in the federal government and they were not subject to alienation by allottees. Houses were built by the government for the Indians, and the efforts of government and missionary forces, often operating in close cooperation, were directed toward making the Kiowa Apache self-supporting, individualistic agricultural entrepreneurs. It was the philosophy of the government at this time that the process of acculturation could be accomplished by putting the Indian on an individual, property-holding basis. The presumption was that self-interest, thrift and self-respect would follow, and soon the Indian's way of life would become like that of his white rural neighbors of Western European extraction.

Thus, within a period of three decades the very foundations of the old way of life of the Kiowa Apache were shattered and in its place the Indians were offered the foreign culture and value system of the white men who had engulfed them. In the circumstances it would be indeed surprising if their reaction was not to reassert and reaffirm the values of the old way of life. This they did by means of the Ghost

---

[22] *Annual Report of the Commissioner of Indian Affairs to the Secretary of the Interior for 1900* (Washington: U.S. Government Printing Office), p. 333.

Dance. This messianic, revivalistic religious cult diffused into the area in the early 1890's and persisted until about 1910, though it waned and faded out gradually after the turn of the century, owing to white pressure as well as the Indians' disappointment over the failure of its prophecies to materialize.

The Ghost Dance religion originated through the dreams of a Paviotso Indian named Wovoka, who in a period of illness and stress had visions of the white men being destroyed by a great holocaust, the Indian dead returning to life, the old hunting preserves once more abounding with game, and the Indians returning to their ancient, pre-white way of life. This cult diffused rapidly throughout the Plains in the 1890's, coinciding with the destruction of aboriginal Indian cultures in the area consequent upon the westward movement and accompanying depredations of white settlers. Initially it was taken up with great hope and enthusiasm among the Kiowa and associated Kiowa Apache. But the Ghost Dance, with its promise of a return to the "golden age" of an unrestricted nomadic life, did not last. The old way of life was hopelessly shattered. There was no tangible evidence to which the Indians could tie their yearning for a return to the aboriginal way of life. The Kiowa dispatched one of their members to investigate the source of the new religion. He traveled north and westward, on horseback, by railroad and on foot, until he reached the camp of the prophet Wovoka. Upon his return he announced that he found the dreamer to be an ordinary Indian leading a quite secular existence much as the rest of his tribesmen. The Ghost Dance was declared a fraud by leaders among the Kiowa and Kiowa Apache. Kiowa Apache informants old enough to remember these events insisted that the news brought back by the Kiowa "pilgrim" was decisive in turning their people away from the cult. Nonetheless, Ghost Dances were held sporadically until 1910, usually under the sponsorship of a Kiowa faction, but with attendance from the Kiowa Apache. Finally, in disillusion and because of missionary and government pressures, the Indians ceased practicing the Ghost Dance religion.

Antedating the Ghost Dance, but continuing during its period of existence and surviving it, was another form of revivalistic religious expression, the well-known peyote cult. Since the peyote cult forms an important part of contemporary Kiowa Apache culture we shall discuss it further in that context.

3

TODAY the Kiowa Apache number about four hundred persons according to the census figures[23] of the Western Oklahoma Consolidated Indian Agency at Anadarko, Oklahoma. It must, however, be borne in mind that for census purposes the Indian Service defines a Kiowa Apache as any person so enrolled. This means, with the frequency of intertribal marriages and varying degrees of white admixture, that many of these individuals are offspring of marriages in which only one spouse is Kiowa Apache, and then perhaps only one-half so. Some have dual enrollment. Indian parents are permitted to enroll their children in the tribe of either parent and in some cases in both, although the latter practice is discouraged in order to prevent individuals from claiming double shares of annuities or other benefits that might result from the settlement of old treaty claims.

These people are concentrated in two communities, one approximately five miles west of Fort Cobb, the other about six miles west of Apache, both in Caddo County, southwestern Oklahoma. Their land allotments are spread over a much wider area, however, for most individuals prefer to live with relatives rather than on their own allotments.

The two communities are not entirely Kiowa Apache. The residences of these Indians are interspersed among those of rural whites, Kiowas, Comanches and a few Negroes.

Most of the present-day Kiowa Apache know English. Among those under about forty years of age English is rapidly becoming the major language of everyday affairs. The old people have a lesser command of English and tend to use the native language among themselves. Individuals of the younger generations can understand Kiowa Apache but tend to speak it haltingly and very imperfectly, employing English words freely when they cannot recall native words. Children know only English, and it seems to be merely a matter of time—perhaps another generation or two—before the native language will be replaced entirely by English. In their contacts with

[23] The time referred to, in what follows, is 1949–50, when a general ethnographic study of the Kiowa Apache was conducted and Jim Whitewolf's life history was recorded. The sociocultural situation here described should not, therefore, be regarded as obtaining in all particulars now, although it is the writer's belief that it holds true in all major respects.

Indians of other tribes the Kiowa Apache usually employ English. In the event of intertribal contacts of old people who know no English, the tendency is to use Comanche, which has become a sort of Indian *lingua franca* because it has the reputation of being very easy to learn.

The Kiowa Apache settlements are reached from Fort Cobb and Apache by sand-bedded motor roads which are extremely poor in wet weather. The road from Apache westward is somewhat better than that leading from Fort Cobb, being occasionally graveled. Road graders are in constant operation on both roads in an effort to keep them passable. Frequently, however, when the weather is wet, these roads become veritable seas of mud, with the result that the Kiowa Apache of both communities are temporarily cut off from the shopping centers of their nearest towns unless they walk a round-trip total of ten to twelve miles and carry their goods. As there is no public transportation service to the two towns from their homes, a large proportion of the Indians own automobiles, ranging from broken-down "jalopies" of the 1930's to the latest in Chevrolets, Fords, and in a few cases, more expensive models. In dry weather the roads are good and one may see at almost any hour of the day or night the choking clouds of dust stirred up by their cars as they drive to town, dances, to churches, peyote meetings and on visits.

Their dwellings are typically old wooden houses, seldom having more than four or five rooms, in very bad repair. Most of these houses were built by the government at the turn of the century or shortly thereafter, when the old reservation was allotted individually. Furniture usually consists of a kitchen wood-burning stove, several beds, a straight wooden chair or two, and occasionally an old broken-down sofa. Rugs, curtains and similar items are usually lacking. An occasional old photograph of deceased relatives or prominent members of the tribe in the past graces the walls in most of the Kiowa Apache homes. None of the homes have running water or an inside toilet, and only a small minority have electricity. A few have battery-operated radios and some receive newspapers by rural airplane delivery. None has a telephone.

Nearly every household has a garden, an acre or two in size, in which corn, watermelons, potatoes and other vegetables are grown for home use. A few families engage in farming and cattle raising on a market scale. Most of these, however, have assured incomes from farm leases and/or oil royalties, and the farming which is carried on is conducted in an uneconomic manner. Often, unneeded equipment is purchased, and records of costs and income are kept poorly or not at all. Such activity is apparently carried on for prestige purposes more than for any economic reasons. The Kiowa Apache have never become serious, successful farmers, and future prospects of this do not appear great. There are cases in which individuals, dissatisfied with a meager income from agricultural leases, have gathered together funds to obtain needed equipment and expressed a determination to enter into farming, only to allow the equipment to rust and fall into disrepair as they turned to some other economic expedient.

In the spring of 1949, a movement was under way to organize a cooperative farm-credit organization, largely in the Fort Cobb community. Several such associations have existed in various areas under the agency's jurisdiction, some rather successfully, in the past. A number of the younger Kiowa Apache veterans, returning from the Second World War and beginning to face economic responsibilities of their own, manifested most of the interest shown in establishing such a credit association in their community. Such associations are organized by the Indians in cooperation with the Indian Service and its agricultural agent. Once formed, the association borrows a lump sum for capitalization from the government at one per cent interest. The association then loans the money to its members at three per cent for a six-year term. Eligibility qualifications are established by the government. The Indian borrower must show evidence that he has land on which he can carry out farming operations. In general, this is accomplished by what is called a "non-disturbance agreement," whereby the prospective farmer gets the consent of someone owning land, usually a relative, to farm a portion of it. The Indian Service farm agent, together with the Agricultural Extension Service officials and the officers of the credit association, screen applications for loans. Once granted the loan, the Indian is given purchase orders for the equipment, seed and fertilizers that he requires. No actual money is transferred into his hands. All stock and equipment that the individual Indians receive is inalienable and cannot be disposed of without prior consent of the government. The difference between the association's borrowing and lending rates of interest is intended to cover operating expenses and to absorb any defaults on loan payment. When all loans are retired, such an association will have a common fund of its own to meet emergency needs of its members.

In 1949 the negotiations for organization of such a credit association among the Kiowa Apache had not proceeded far enough to provide a basis for prediction of its success or failure. A certain amount of bickering and criticism among individuals concerned was observed and it seemed likely that the internal politics of such an organization would to some extent become enmeshed with long-standing jealousies and ill feelings among individuals and families that stem from wealth differences, disputes over women and similar matters. Whether this could split the group apart and destroy its functioning remained to be seen.

The great majority of the Kiowa Apache have no regular gainful occupations. Their incomes are obtained from the leasing of their allotment lands for agriculture or for petroleum extraction by oil corporations. Such incomes vary a great deal from person to person. Those whose incomes are derived solely from agricultural leasing receive but a few hundred dollars a year. They constitute the majority. The few who are fortunate enough to have land that is producing oil get very large incomes in oil royalties, often several hundred dollars a month. In two cases the monthly income is over two thousand dollars.

It is interesting to note that such wealth differences are not particularly reflected in the appearance or upkeep of homes. The few Kiowa Apache with rather large incomes purchase expensive furniture and household appliances to some extent, but these rapidly deteriorate from lack of upkeep or proper use. One of the wealthy individuals with an income in excess of two thousand dollars a month maintains a house in a nearby small city and a ranch in the vicinity of Apache. The ranch is conducted uneconomically; expensive equipment is purchased on personal whim. This person also maintains, for purposes of prestige, a race horse which he enters at the annual fair. This animal costs about one hundred dollars a month in training and feeding expenses during the spring and summer seasons. A large group of this man's relatives is supported by creating for them various nominal jobs such as plowing, harvesting and chauffeuring.

A few Kiowa Apache men work as farm laborers on occasion, but only sporadically and under the pressure of immediate economic necessity.

Land allotments are the only assets of these people. When we recall that the allotments were given only to those living during 1901–3 and again, in 1908, to those born between 1903–8, it appears that there is a group of Kiowa Apache under the age of forty with serious economic problems. It should be pointed out in this regard that it is virtually impossible for Indians in this area to obtain jobs in the towns, because of lack of qualifications as well as prejudice and discriminatory practices by white employers. Moreover, the few jobs that would be available in nearby towns would not begin to solve the problem.

Actually the younger landless and jobless Kiowa Apache manage to get along, owing to the deep-rooted and pervasive kinship ties and patterns of sharing in the cultural tradition. To refuse a relative's request for material aid or service is to risk severe censure. Observations in the field led to the conclusion that no matter how reprehensible one's conduct, the fact of kinship to the offended person is sufficient to obtain his pardon. To have many relatives and to produce a large family are still very strong values with these people. One who has no kin, or whose marriage has not resulted in progeny, is often spoken of as a poor man.

This is important, for it makes understandable the situation of the younger generations of Kiowa Apache who have no source of income of their own. These people are provided for by the elder group that has land and income from land. For the most part the young people are idle. During the spring, summer and early autumn they travel about a great deal attending dances, softball games and fairs. Someday, they know, the elders will die and they will inherit the land and its income. Their children, in turn, will lead the same kind of unproductive life they have led, until the land passes to them.

The Kiowa Apache younger generations exhibit a restlessness and insecurity in their behavior. This quite frequently results in drunkenness, delinquency, and occasionally in serious crime. There are numerous shifting sexual alliances and brittle marriages. The white world of the nearby towns offers many attractions: the movies, the pool hall, the latest dress styles and permanent waves, liquor illicitly obtained from bootleggers. This requires money. Relatives are accordingly exploited, not without a certain amount of bickering and

ill feeling in many cases. Usually, however, such demands are ful-
filled, even though it means parting with the last dollar in the
house.

The problems connected with land and its utilization are the most
serious ones among the Kiowa Apache today. The entire system of
leasing and of the utilization of lease income forms the heart of their
economic life and is important enough to justify exposition and
analysis at this point.

We shall consider agricultural leasing first. Since 1947 it has been
the policy of the United States Indian Service to allow the individual
Indian to negotiate his own farm leases. The Agency sets down,
however, certain regulations governing the entire procedure. It must
be satisfied that the rental is a fair one to the Indian lessor. The
contract specifies that conservation measures must be observed by
the lessee, that he be responsible for providing insurance for any
insurable buildings on the premises, and that such buildings be
kept in proper repair.

Leases are signed for a five-year period. Payments of rent, at
agreed-upon intervals and amounts, are made directly to the lessor
unless his individual money account at the Agency shows indebted-
ness or shows that he has been ordered to pay alimony or provide
support for minor children. In such cases the rental money is paid
into his account and disbursed by the Agency for such obligations
before any money is placed at his disposal.

Because so many Indians with land have only the meager income
provided by a farm lease on 160 acres, certain practices arise which
create serious problems for the Indian as well as for the Agency.
The chief problem concerns the extension of leases. Quite often a
lessee will pay the Indian lessor the land rent for the entire five-year
period in advance; in other cases he will pay him a large fraction of
it. The Indian is glad to have the money all at once, for usually he is
in debt or has need of the money for some expensive venture, such
as purchasing a car, holding a dance or sponsoring a peyote meeting.
He spends the entire amount in a relatively short time, and upon finding
himself again penniless, he goes to the Agency to request cancellation
of the lease and negotiation of a new one for a period of five years,
in order to extend the expiration date of the original lease and thus
be in a position to obtain more rental money in advance. Many
lessees are perfectly willing to agree to this procedure, since by

extending their lease rights into the future they protect themselves against possible rising land values and higher rents. The Indian lessor, because he is usually in dire need of immediate cash that he can realize by extension, seldom if ever raises the question of higher rent. Cases exist in which the agency, in the interest of the Indian, has insisted on higher rent as a condition of cancellation and extension, only to discover later that the lessee and lessor have entered into a private agreement whereby the increased rent is actually not charged.

As a result of such procedures, the Indian landholder is constantly overspending his income and finding himself without funds and in debt. So long as he is able to continue to extend his leases, he has no incentive or interest in planning any kind of budget of his economic affairs.

In an effort to decrease the frequency of such practices, the Agency has laid down the rule that a bona fide emergency must exist before it will agree to cancellation of a lease. Emergencies must be proved by the Indian and include such items as medical and funeral expenses and repairs to dwellings necessitated by disasters such as floods or hurricanes. Occasionally, desperate for funds, the Indian will persuade an unscrupulous physician, dentist or other professional person to write a certifying letter to the agency authorities stating that he is under care or urgently in need of care, when in fact such is not the case.

The procedures concerning the leasing of land to oil companies are rather different. Over these leases the control of the Indian Service is more complete. Periodically the Agency advertises Indian allotments which are open for competitive bidding for mineral rights. Sealed bids are submitted by interested oil companies. The bidding is on the initial bonus to be offered the lessor, since the rental is fixed by the government at a dollar and a quarter per acre per annum. Once a lease is negotiated, the company pays into the individual account of the Indian lessor at the agency the amount of the bonus. This sum cannot be used by the Indian in any manner or at any time he desires. Instead, a family budget is drawn up for him in consultation with Agency personnel and he receives a monthly check from his account balance. In the event of emergencies he may be allowed to draw additional funds.

The oil lease is made for a period of ten years, with automatic renewal rights by the company concerned unless it has failed to commence drilling operations by the end of the ninth year. The rental of a dollar and a quarter per acre per annum is paid into the Indian's account at the Agency and is disbursed in the same manner as the bonus money. Should oil be struck on the land, the rental ceases and then the Indian is credited periodically with one-eighth of the value of the products. These funds are handled in the same manner as the lease bonus and the rental fees.

At one point a movement was initiated by some of the Indians to secure permission to sell their oil-royalty right of one-eighth of the value of products for an immediate cash consideration. Hitherto it has been Agency policy to permit sale of one-half of oil-royalty rights only in unusual cases of genuine emergency. The sale of oil-royalty rights amounts, of course, to a wager on the Indian's part that his land will not produce oil, or at least that oil will not be found in sufficient quantity for his oil-royalty benefits to exceed the amount he would receive immediately by selling the rights. From the oil company's standpoint, however, the wager in such a transaction is just the reverse. It needs hardly to be pointed out that the oil companies, with their technical staffs and equipment, are in a better position to predict the petroleum potential of a tract of land than are the Indians. The idea of disposing of oil-royalty rights would appear manifestly unwise, yet many Indians desire to do so. This desire is stimulated to some extent by the fact that one or two cases are on record in which the oil company made a mistake in prediction, paid a large sum for oil-royalty rights, and found only a "dry hole," as petroleum prospectors call a non-producing field.

Another device of the Indians to obtain large sums of money at one time is to press for the granting of a fee patent on their lands so that they may sell them outright. It is the policy of the Agency in this regard to remove the governmental restriction on allotments whenever in its judgment the individual Indian is competent to manage his own economic affairs. Again, however, experience has shown that the large amounts realized are frequently spent very rapidly, sometimes not constructively by any criterion, and the Indian is soon again penniless, with neither money nor assets in land.

In all of these dealings with the Indian Service the individual experiences certain frustrations, thwarting of plans, and feelings of dependence and submission to external authority. To a great many of the less acculturated Kiowa Apache the Agency at Anadarko ("the office") is a vast, confusing force, the operations and aims of which they little comprehend. Consequently there are attitudes of hostility and ill feeling toward it and toward the Agency employees with whom they have dealings. A frequent expression by the Indians runs along the lines, "It's *my* land. Those government people just work in an office. They don't have land or know anything about it. I know what's best for myself." In these circumstances it is exceedingly difficult for Agency personnel to convince the individual Apache they are concerned with his best interests.

A most serious problem confronting the Kiowa Apache today, and which will confront them increasingly in the future, concerns the inheritance of land. The population is increasing somewhat; large families are everywhere to be noticed among the younger married couples. As allotments are handed down over the generations, subdivision has resulted in ever larger numbers of increasingly smaller interests. This subdivision seldom takes the form of actual physical division of the land among heirs. Nonetheless, the lease income has to be divided into a large number of small amounts. In a random sample of data on heirship taken to get an idea of the range of numbers of heirs to 160-acre tracts, it was found that cases existed of nineteen persons having equal interests, while a figure of five to ten heirs was rather common. When one realizes that three to five hundred dollars per year is a typical agricultural rental for a 160-acre plot the individual income can be seen to be appallingly low.

In many cases an individual owns fractional interests in several scattered allotments bequeathed to him by various kin. This of course makes agricultural operations impossible for him even if he has a desire to become a farmer. At the present time the Indian Service in the area is experimenting with a program of land consolidation, by means of which fractional scattered interests can be traded so that each individual will have a single block of land. The hope is that through the farm credit cooperative associations mentioned earlier such individuals can be encouraged to enter agriculture.

From our discussion the difficult economic situation of these Indians may be seen. The land is their only asset. If it is alienated or if the mineral rights are sold, they are faced with almost certain poverty. To permit without limitation or restriction the practice of cancellation and extension of leases means continued insecurity for the Indian and the utter impossibility of enlisting his interest in any form of planning of his economic affairs. In most cases the Indian's income is barely sufficient for minimal maintenance of himself and his dependents, despite the fact that he is entitled to (though not obliged to use) the free medical care of the Indian Service, is exempt from property taxes, and has no housing rent to pay.

His economic condition is further complicated by his value system and the choices it suggests in expending income. Sponsorship of a three-day dance, at which the host provides the food for a large number of guests, is a very expensive venture; it may consume a large portion of a year's farm-lease income. While there does not appear to be any evidence that failure to do so occasionally will entail a serious loss of prestige in the eyes of the community, many an individual seems to sponsor such gatherings in the desire to attract the eyes of the community to himself and to be thought of as a " good and generous person." Again, membership in the peyote cult imposes upon a Kiowa Apache the obligation of occasional sponsorship of a peyote meeting, which costs forty to fifty dollars. Ownership of an automobile is virtually a necessity because of distances from centers where supplies can be purchased. It is also a matter of prestige. The tendency is to purchase a new car if possible. Failure to maintain automobiles properly, plus the rapid deterioration due to bad roads, makes their upkeep very expensive. All of these ways of expending very limited incomes spell almost constant bankruptcy for the great majority of Kiowa Apache who do not have the good fortune, as do a few, of receiving large incomes from oil royalties.

The view of the Indian Service is that entry into agriculture is the only possible avenue of the Indian to an increased steady income, with security for the future. We have already alluded to the unsuccessful efforts in the historic past to make farmers of the Kiowa Apache. In this connection it is necessary to underscore the fact that the sedentary existence associated with an agricultural economy is totally foreign to these people. Despite the fact that a very great deal of the aboriginal culture—religion and ceremonial, hunt and raid, various folk beliefs and customs—is gone and all but forgotten, the psychology of nomadism, the restless impulse to be on the move, the strong tendency toward individualism and inability to cooperate in a context exceeding the bounds of the extended family group, are today very strong. One cannot fail to get the impression from association with the Kiowa Apache that they are most happy when they are in motion. The amount of travel in automobiles, to visit and to attend dances and peyote meetings, often over long distances and for many days at a time, is phenomenal. Undoubtedly these traits have roots in the old way of life. It does not seem far-fetched to say that the automobile is the present-day analogue of the horse in Kiowa Apache culture. The marked tendency toward individualism, while rooted in the aboriginal status system that emphasized individual achievements and encouraged boasting, unquestionably is fed and sustained by the insecurities and hostilities engendered by the present-day sociocultural situation. These factors present extraordinarily great difficulties to any program designed to make the contemporary Kiowa Apache a successful sedentary farming people.

To the Kiowa Apache themselves the serious economic problems that may be objectively delineated by the outside observer do not appear as problems at all, except to a very few highly acculturated, relatively well educated individuals. One encounters very frequently the Indian attitude that "the government will always take care of us." Despite frequent and bitter expressions of deep dissatisfaction with, and hostility to, the Indian Service and its policies and programs, to a great many Indians the very thought of the complete withdrawal of the Service from management and control of their affairs, of being "turned loose," as the phrase goes, gives rise to acute feelings of anxiety. Their dependence is indeed very strong, objectively and psychologically.

KIOWA APACHE children attend the public schools in or near their communities. The people living west of Fort Cobb send their children to the school in that town. A school bus is in regular operation, stopping for the children in the mornings near their homes and returning them there in the late afternoons. Lunches are available at the school at nominal cost.

The children of the Indians living west of the town of Apache attend elementary school at the tiny settlement of Boone, around which their homes are located. Boone consists of two small grocery stores, which also dispense gasoline, and the elementary school building. This school provides education through the eighth grade. The closest high school facilities are in the town of Apache. One hundred twenty-six pupils attended the Boone school at the time of research, of whom 68 per cent were Indian, mostly Kiowa Apache.

There are four school rooms, each combining two grades, and there are three teachers and a principal. The principal combines with his administrative duties the teaching of seventh and eighth grades. Around the school building is a schoolyard with rather rudimentary play equipment.

The impression gained from informal interviews is that these educators, while competent in their subjects, are entirely lacking in interest in Indian children and their peculiar cultural background. They are also rather poorly paid. Their attitudes toward the Indians are much like those of the white community: "Indians are a funny lot and you just can't do much with them."

The major problem concerning the Indian pupils, in the opinion of the teachers, is attendance, which is extremely irregular. Frequently girls are kept out of school to assist at home with laundering, care of small children and other family chores. In the springtime Kiowa Apache boys absent themselves from school to pick wild pecans, which they sell in order to get spending money. Many children get a late start in school in the autumn, due to the many dances and powwows their families attend. Until the weather becomes too inclement for such events to be held, autumn attendance is very irregular.

The interest of Kiowa Apache parents in the school and its work is very slight. Apart from the annual Christmas program and one or two other social events to which they are invited, they seldom visit the school. There was no Parent-Teacher Association or similar group at the time of field work. When a child's school attendance becomes seriously irregular, the school principal usually sends a note to the parents, advising them to see that the child attends school more consistently. Occasionally the principal receives a scribbled note from parents asking him to whip a child in order to improve the child's attendance record. It is not without significance culturally that such a request is made of the school official and that the parent does not inflict such punishment himself. The writer never saw a child physically punished among the Kiowa Apache; the mores oppose it strongly. Kiowa Apache children are indulged to a degree that many whites would call "spoiled rotten." It is somewhat surprising that parents even ask the school principal to mete out physical punishment. Actually, however, the school principal rarely resorts to such measures, and only as a final expedient when other means fail.

On the positive side, the Kiowa Apache children seem to excel in athletics and in art work. Their achievements in athletics earn for the Indians some commendation and praise from the whites of the area, whose general attitudes toward Indians are rather negative and derogatory. In the academic subjects Kiowa Apache children manifest only moderate interest, and as a group they do not do as well as white children. It is not surprising that they show no interest in 4-H Club work such as raising vegetable gardens and learning conservation practices. The curriculum as a whole is geared to white interests and backgrounds, not those of Indians.

Although school personnel claimed that no marked feelings of difference were manifested between Indian and white children in the school situation, observation of informal play groups in the schoolyard indicated noticeable separatism.

With regard to opportunities for higher education, the Indian Service makes educational loans, usually for vocational training, but not excluding liberal-arts education, to those young people who can meet the requirements. These include high scores on aptitude and intelligence tests, strong recommendations, and a definite vocational objective. Loans are initially made for one year, with continued assistance depending upon the student's record and the availability of funds in the Indian Service budget. The student must begin to repay his loan, on a monthly basis with interest, within ninety days after graduation. The stringency of these requirements, the great uncertainty of obtaining employment after training is completed, and the hesitancy about leaving the domestic fold for a strange new situation have had the result that only six Kiowa Apache have applied for and received such loans in the past fifteen years, and not all of these completed their training.

THE ABORIGINAL Kiowa Apache religious concepts and practices, centering in the acquisition of supernatural power and its use in shamanistic curing rites, are gone in practice and only generally remembered by the older people. The white man's medicine, in the institutional form of Indian Service hospitals and clinics, and the peyote cult, of which we shall speak presently, have supplanted the old methods of curing. No Kiowa Apache today practices shamanism. A few individuals are reputed to have "power," and accounts were obtained of an occasional shamanistic rite being attempted as recently as about 1945. Among the closely associated Kiowa Indians a few shamans still function, and a few Kiowa Apache today patronize them occasionally. When they do, the curing rite is usually carried on in the context of a peyote meeting and the shaman is paid in cash. Fees range from seven to twelve dollars.

Religion for the present-day Kiowa Apache centers in three institutions: the Baptist Church, the Methodist Church, and the Native American (peyote) Church.

Near Boone, Oklahoma, there is a small Methodist Church, whose congregation and pastor are Indian. The Fort Cobb group of Kiowa Apache had no Methodist Church building at the time of field research. There the Indians conducted their services on a regular rotational basis from week to week in private homes. A fund-raising drive was in progress to build a Methodist Church in the Fort Cobb community, by means of pledges, donations and "free-will offerings."

A minority of the Kiowa Apache are Baptists. They attend a small church near Fort Cobb. This church also is all-Indian in membership and has an Indian pastor and assistant pastor.

A large proportion, perhaps a majority, of the adult Kiowa Apache men are devotees of the Native American Church, an Indian cult centering around the eating of peyote, a mildly psychedelic cactus which produces feelings of exhilaration and sometimes color visions. Although women are not strictly prohibited from attending the peyote meetings, they do so infrequently. However, they play a major role in the feasting and social gatherings that follow peyote meetings. The Native American Church since 1918 has been a chartered religious body under the laws of Oklahoma. It has local branches, or "chapters," throughout the state. Peyote cult practice will be described later in this chapter.

In the Baptist and Methodist Churches activities consist of regular Sunday morning services, occasional summer encampments, and frequent evening prayer meetings at the homes of the members. The Sunday services are conventional in form and content, usually consisting of a sermon in English by the pastor on selected portions of the Bible, with rather homely examples on how the precepts apply to daily life, followed by group singing of hymns. Some of the hymns are translations into the native language of traditional church songs. The prayer meetings take place in response to a request by a member of the congregation for prayer to aid the recovery of a sick relative. Summer camp meetings, in addition to the daily gatherings for worship and conduct of church business affairs, provide an opportunity for visiting and general social intercourse in a physical setting that is especially congenial to the older generations who remember the days of the tipi and the outdoor life.

The moral injunctions of the Baptist Church are considerably stricter than those of the Methodists. The exhortations are frequent, intense and lengthy against such "worldly" activities as dancing in all forms, drinking alcoholic beverages, and smoking. This evokes some conflicts in the minds of members, particularly in relation to the Indian dances. Although these dances as practiced today have no religious significance and are looked upon by the Indians as purely social "good times," the Baptist Church looks upon them as heathen and sinful in nature. Nonetheless, a good many of the church members and their children attend them and remain secretive about such participation as far as the church is concerned.

A marked difference between Methodists and Baptists lies in their respective attitudes toward the third religious group, that of the Native American Church. The Methodist Church is tolerant, or at least indifferent in the matter. Indeed, many if not most of the Kiowa Apache Methodists are ardent peyotists. There is no objection to this on the part of the Methodist pastors. In fact, the present minister of the church near Boone has in the past belonged to the peyote cult. His attitude and reason for no longer participating are given in the following excerpt from an interview with the writer:

> The peyote religion doesn't do any harm and I am not opposed to it. I used to take part in it eight or ten years ago and I am still a member of the Native American Church. My only criticism is that it doesn't have a firm foundation and doesn't help the Indians to progress. It should be organized on a better basis. . . . I think we should be proud of our Indian religion. . . .
>
> There is absolutely no question about that [i.e., the power of peyote to cure illness—C.S.B.]. It does have that power. I took part in the peyote religion and I know that. Peyote has an effect on you. . . . It's a feeling that makes you want to pray, a religious feeling.

Though peyote meetings most commonly occur on Saturday nights and last well into the following morning, they do not interfere with church attendance seriously because they are held at irregular intervals, often many weeks apart. Kiowa Apaches who participate in both the Methodist Church and the peyote cult feel no conflict at all. Both are considered "worships," and therefore good. The prevalent attitude is that the more religious activity one can take part in, the better.

The serious religious division among these people involves Baptists versus peyotists. The Baptists consider the peyote religion to be paganism and idolatry. In their view peyote is a physically and morally harmful drug, and they would like nothing better than to see the use of peyote outlawed. In 1949 students from Oklahoma Baptist University participated in a radio broadcast in which they condemned peyote as a major deterrent to the progress of the Indians. Highly irate, the peyotists among the Kiowa Apache and Kiowa lost no time in securing an opportunity to reply over the same radio station. Two weeks after the broadcast by the Baptist students one of their best educated and most capable spokesmen gave an answer for the Native American Church to the Baptist charges. There is no love lost between Baptists and peyotists among the Kiowa Apache; verbal recriminations are strong and bitter. Jim Whitewolf, who participated in the Methodist Church and was also a most ardent devotee of the peyote cult, characterized the Baptists as "too much Christian people."

The peyote religion among the Kiowa Apache dates from approximately 1880, when it diffused into the area from the southwest. It was taken up with great ardor and today persists as the most vital religious force in the group.

A brief description of the peyote-cult practices is in order at this point.[24] A meeting may begin anytime after sundown but before midnight and it lasts until shortly after sunrise. The meeting takes place in a tipi specially erected for the occasion. The participants sit on the ground in a circle around a fire. To the accompaniment of a gourd rattle and drum each member takes a turn singing conventionalized peyote songs. Periodically prayers are addressed to "God" and to "Jesus" asking for health and long life. The devotees eat the

---

[24] For a fully detailed description of the Kiowa Apache peyote cult, as well as some general sociological observations concerning it, see the writer's "Peyotism among the Kiowa-Apache and Neighboring Tribes," in *Southwestern Journal of Anthropology*, 6: 2 (1950), 212–22.

dried tops of peyote plants (*Lophophora williamsii*), a mildly intoxicating, apparently non-habit-forming substance, which sometimes causes the subject to have color visions. At midnight there is a ritualized water-drinking ceremony, and at dawn a peyote "breakfast" is served, consisting of water, pemmican, dried corn and corn-meal mush. The general ideology of the peyote religion is that God placed the peyote plant on earth so that the Indian, poor and illiterate, could enter into communion with him by eating it. An attitude of mystical awe and reverence is displayed toward peyote and to it is attributed power to cure almost any illness to which mankind is heir.

Observation of religious activities among the present-day Kiowa Apache Indians leads to the conclusion that the peyote cult is by far the most meaningful and valued form of religious expression and is functionally related to the total sociocultural pattern. The peyote religion serves as an emotional outlet, as a cohesive force in a situation which is generally characterized by family and group rivalries, economic insecurities and marked health anxieties.

FORMAL political structure, never strong or well defined in Kiowa Apache society, scarcely exists today. There are no recognized chiefs and no individual makes any claim to such status in the tribe. One wealthy individual, prominent in Kiowa Apache peyotism and very active in intertribal ceremonials of the modern variety, has allegedly claimed to represent the tribe in such matters as "chief," but such title, if indeed it was actually used, was certainly self-arrogated.

In their relations as a body with the Indian Service, the Kiowa Apache participate together with the Kiowa and Comanche in an intertribal council. The Kiowa Apache elect two representatives known as the "Apache Business Committee" who meet monthly with elected representatives of the other two tribes and with the superintendent of the Agency and his staff. The election of the Kiowa Apache council members occurs every four years. Voting is open to all members of the tribe who are twenty-one years of age or older. The total intertribal council, consisting of five Kiowa members, five Comanche, and two Kiowa Apache, is subdivided into committees for various matters; these committees include Land and Resources, Recreation, Medical, Loans, Education and Claims. The function of these committees is to make reports and recommendations to the council as a whole, which in turn discusses them with the Indian Service officials. Neither the committees nor the council as a whole has the power, however, to act on its own. Each can only suggest and recommend. Final decisions always rest with the Indian Service. There was no evidence to suggest that the rank and file of the tribe take any particular interest in the activities of the council, except in the matter of claims against the government. In connection with claims there is a great amount of lively discussion and opinion, for every Kiowa Apache is always interested in the possibility of realizing income from the settlement of such claims.

INADEQUATE sanitation and lack of knowledge results in a high rate of illness among these people today. Pneumonia and tuberculosis of the pulmonary tract have been especially prevalent, as have also trachoma and related eye diseases. There have been several cases of alcoholism and venereal disease. Improper diet, especially among children, leads to various nutritional deficiency diseases and to poor teeth.

The Indian Service maintains outpatient clinics and a large hospital in the general area, where the Kiowa Apache may receive free treatment and hospitalization. But the existence of such facilities does not automatically meet the problem. Among the Indians there is a deep-seated distrust of these government medical facilities and a marked reluctance to use them. In the early days of Indian administration these facilities had the reputation of being staffed by personnel who were not always fully competent and who made no effort whatever to understand the Indian patient entering what was to him a very strange situation. Members of the older generations, wedded to native curing concepts and practices, went to the white man's hospital only as a last resort. Soon the hospital got the reputation of being a place where one went to die. The dread with which the Kiowa Apache view death and places associated with death did not help to make the government hospital popular among them, to say the least. This feeling has persisted, and many Kiowa Apache of the present day who know nothing of aboriginal curing and who accept white medicine prefer to become indebted to a private physician rather than use the Indian Service medical facilities. Moreover, the medical centers of the Indian Service are understaffed, the hospital is usually crowded, and much delay and red tape must be gone through in order to receive care. Another deterrent is distance; clinics and hospitals are many miles from the Indians' homes, farther than the shops and stores. All of these factors conspire against the good health of the Kiowa Apache. Infant mortality is high; hardly a family known to the writer has not lost at least one baby, and many large families have lost several. Many adults are chronically ill with various disorders.

THE CONTEMPORARY picture that emerges from our discussion is not a happy or promising one. It is of a people between two cultural worlds, the old one irretrievably gone and to a large extent forgotten, the new one foreign and little understood, engulfing them, involving them, but not truly embracing them and being meaningfully embraced by them. The present-day Kiowa Apache are a people without a stable pattern of existence. They lack a set of traditional, well-defined, meaningful productive roles. They live on the fringe of the white man's economy, gaining their inadequate livelihood from an exchange arrangement of the market economy whereby the white man obtains use of an important factor in production, the land. Apart from the routine details of procedure in establishing and maintaining this relationship, the Indian scarcely comprehends the complex socioeconomic and technical processes whereby he receives money in exchange for the right of exploitation of the surface and subterranean riches of his land. Without well-defined, meaningful and valued roles and goals in life, with a cultural tradition that disinclines him toward a settled way of life, the contemporary Kiowa Apache spends most of his waking life at Indian dances, in informal conversation and gossip with other Indians, and at the Indian Agency constantly arranging and rearranging his economic affairs with the aim of realizing the most money in his pocket at one time.[25] Subordinated as he is by the white man's world about him, he keeps his inner anxieties and frustrations contained within himself. When he can obtain liquor—forbidden to him both by state and federal

[25] This outlook can be related to aboriginal patterns. In the pre-white hunting and gathering economy, food was usually obtained in quantity and there was always a store on hand sufficient to maintain the family camp between hunting expeditions. The need to be concerned daily about where the next meal was coming from did not exist in the aboriginal way of life.

laws—he usually drinks to excess and forgets his problems temporarily. The peyote religion is a major means of self-expression. Here, in communion with his fellows, under the stimulating influence of peyote, the Kiowa Apache is periodically able to get release, to give vent to his repressed fears, anxieties and sorrows over his health and welfare and that of his relatives. Having addressed fervent prayers to "God" and "Jesus," whom he has come to identify to some extent with the native concept of Creator, he comes away from the intimate, primary-group atmosphere of the peyote meeting feeling reinvigorated, with a fresh store of hope for the future. His situation is again bearable, at least until the next peyote meeting. So life carries on.

As long as the Indian is able to eke out a bare living by the land-leasing arrangements, and as long as the younger generation has little prospect for employment of any skills its members might acquire through education, so long, it appears, will the present pattern continue.

I

Early Years

I WAS BORN on the north side of Spring Creek, which is about one mile southwest of what is now Fort Cobb, Oklahoma. My mother told me I was born there. It was about 1878. Before me there were two brothers, but they died.

Before I was born my father went and talked with the older people. My father approached another old man because of the death of my two brothers. It was the tradition of the older people when children had died in a family. He told the chief,[1] "If it is all right with you, when this baby is born we are going to break the family camp from where we are now. The day he is born we are going to move across the creek. The whole family camp will move across the creek and leave the baby and the old lady there, for a whole day. After that day, the whole camp will come back after the old woman and the baby. She will pray that day that the baby may live to be an old person."[2]

From that day on my folks took care of me and raised me. They said that in years to come they would do something for me.

When I was about six years old I didn't yet have a name.[3] They just called me "boy." Then my father approached some older people

[1] The term *chief* refers to the leader of an encampment composed of several extended families. Selection was achieved by an informally reached agreement among the men. The important qualities were demonstrated ability in warfare and hunting. In a stable hunting and gathering society such as the Kiowa Apache, age was more or less equated with experience and wisdom in the traditional occupations; leaders, therefore, were normally chosen from the older, respected men.

[2] Whether this practice was always followed in families which had lost young children is unknown. However, it is very much in accord with the anxiety felt by Kiowa Apache concerning survival of newborn.

[3] The Kiowa Apache typically delayed the conferral of a name upon a child; if the child died after being named, that name could not be used again, owing to the strong tabu upon uttering the name of a deceased relative. Only when the family felt reasonably certain that the child would survive was a name given.

and told them his boy was growing up and that he wanted someone to name him. An old man said, "We will give you a name." They were going to put up a big tipi and have a feast. At that time they would pray, too. My father said to the old man[4] who was to name me, "I am going to give you a bald-faced horse." On the morning of the day they were going to name me, the old man called all the older people to come into my mother's tipi, and said, "We are going to pray and give this boy a name." All the old people came into the tipi and sat down. The old man who was going to give me a name was sitting so he would be facing the tipi door, looking east. When they got ready to start, my mother brought me inside. I went all around the tipi and sat down on the north side.[5] The old man said, "Now we are going to give this young man a name." My father was seated by this old man. My father got up and said that he wished his son to take the name of his mother's brother. This uncle of my father was already dead. It was the tradition that the name should go on in the family line.[6] That name was Whitewolf.

After the name was given to me, the old man pointed to another old man seated on the south side of the tipi. This old man picked me up, held me in front of him, and raised me up and repeated the name four times.[7] He said, "From this day on you shall be known as Whitewolf, and everybody will know you by that name." Then everyone there took me and lifted me up four times the same way and said the same thing, until I got back around to my mother. When I got back to my mother, the old man who gave me the name took me outside the tipi and he announced in a loud voice to the whole camp, "Today we have named this child Whitewolf, so that you shall all know him by that name. May he grow to be an old man." Then the

[4] Customary practice was that the older members of the family asked an old man, usually a relative, who had a reputation for conferring "good" (that is, auspicious) names, to do so. A "good" name might be one derived from an important hunting or war feat. Names were felt to have supernatural significance; a person who experienced misfortune or grave illness might change his name afterward.

[5] It was a widespread trait of the Plains culture area to erect tipis with the doorway facing east, the direction of the rising sun. In the Kiowa Apache naming ceremony, the honored elder chosen to confer the name sat on the west side with the child to his left and the audience to his right.

[6] This is clearly an instance of deviant practice and may reflect the influence of white acculturation.

[7] Four is a ritual or sacred number.

old man and I came back into the tipi and took our places again.
Then my mother and her mother brought food inside the tipi. When
the feast was over that was the end of it and everyone went back to
his camp. From then on I had my name.

W HEN I WAS about ten, the Kiowas were having a Sun Dance[8] on the
other side of Mountain View—west of it. My father took me there
because he wanted me to grow.[9] It was the morning of the dance
that my father took me. My father had a buffalo hide over him, with
a stick or something holding the hide up over his head. He was
carrying me in front of him. There were many others there who had
brought their children for the same purpose. They all went around
in a line where the Sun Dance was being held. When my father and
I came around to the door of the dance lodge, my father went inside
and I went back to my mother. I guess that was the last time the
Kiowas ever had that ceremony.

From then on, I was getting to be a young man and was going
around among my people.

Then one time my father took me over about a mile west of
Hatchetville, near Cache Creek, to a ceremony. It was called *kotizi*,
water-medicine ceremony. It was in a tipi. My father was already
inside when my mother brought me to the door. I went inside and
sat down. The man who was head of the ceremony prayed for all
the children and he prayed for me. At noon they were feasting inside
the tipi. Over the fire was corn, which was boiling together with
tongue. An old woman was watching this corn and tongue that was
cooking. The people in there had bowls made of turtle shell. Some of
them were of wood. The old woman was dipping the food out with
a buffalo-horn spoon. She gave food to everybody in the tipi and

---

[8] "During the time of the annual Kiowa Sun Dance, the Kiowa-Apache
functioned as a 'band' of the Kiowa, occupying a fixed place on the north side
of the camp circle. During this dance the Kiowa-Apache were said to be under
the jurisdiction of the Kiowa chief. . . ." (J. Gilbert McAllister, "Kiowa-Apache
Social Organization," in F. Eggan [ed.], *Social Anthropology of North American
Tribes* [Chicago, 1937], p. 100.) The Sun Dance, like many other features of their
culture, was learned by the Kiowa Apache only after they reached the Plains,
probably about 250 years ago, and came under the influence of Plains tribes.

[9] The Sun Dance was, among other things, an expression of veneration of the
sun as the source of life and the promoter of growth and well-being of all living
things.

also to the people on the outside. They had just ordinary bowls. There were songs and prayers at this ceremony. The prayers were for the little children to grow. They had done that from way back, a long time ago.

WEST OF ANADARKO, I saw my first Ghost Dance.[10] It was when I was about twelve years old. There were Kiowas, Arapahoes and some of the Apaches. They said that it was the Arapaho up north who had seen the Ghost Dance. They were the ones who brought it down this way. The Arapaho were told when they learned the Ghost Dance that some day they would see all the dead come back to life. They said that those who don't believe in the Ghost Dance will be under the ground, but those that believe will be above. Everybody came into the camp. My mother and father were there. They danced four days. On a certain song everyone in the camp would cry and look up and say, "When are you coming down? Come down to us soon." After the dance, we went back home. The Apaches were camping east of Big Joe's place, along the creek. They were going to have a Ghost Dance. They usually had one every week then. All the tribes around were having the Ghost Dance then. Several years after that, the Apaches began to think that there was nothing to it. I don't know just why. The things they said didn't come true, so they didn't think that there was anything to it. They quit having it after that.

The Kiowas were going to have a Ghost Dance. They said that this was going to be the real one. Some of the Apache went over there. The Kiowas told them what they were going to do. They showed us how to do it. Then we went over to Hatchetville and we were going to do the Ghost Dance the way the Kiowas showed us. There weren't many people there. I was a grown man then, so I went over there on horseback. I went inside. I sat down in back. They all had rattles of cow-hooves that they were shaking. It was something like the Holiness Church of today. They stomped their feet and rolled around on the floor. There was a Kiowa man there running it. He told them that when they finished smoking, he was going up to heaven and see Jesus. They all began to sing after his talk and some of them were saying, "This fellow is going up to see Jesus." Some of them asked for a pillow for this fellow. They said that while he was dancing he was going to fall back, and he should

[10] See Introduction, pp. 16–17.

have a pillow for that. They said his heart would then go up to Jesus. This Kiowa fellow tied a black handkerchief around his wrist. He told them to sing a certain song and that when they did it would take him to heaven. They sang that song. This fellow was kind of grunting. He got stiff and fell backwards and lay there. He lay there about ten or fifteen minutes. Everybody was still singing. After they were through singing, they said they would smoke. After they smoked, he started grunting, and some of them said, "He has come back from heaven." He got up and they gave him a pipe to smoke. Then he laid it back down. They asked him to tell them about his journey to heaven. He said, "When I fell back, I started going up there. I found out where the dead Apaches were and went over to them. I saw Rabbit Shoulder. I shook hands with him. The rest of them were all seated around. He asked me why I came. I said I came for the Apaches, that they had sent me. 'Don't you see them? Look down there, where they are camping. The Apache people sent me here to see you. They want you to see Jesus and have Him come and talk with me.' The old Apache man, Rabbit Shoulder, called for Jesus and told Him I had come to see Him. I saw Jesus coming toward me, and He was a good-looking man. I shook hands with Him. He asked me why I came, and I told Him the Apache people sent me. I told Him to look down and He would see them. I told Him that they want to know when their kinfolk are coming back down to them. They want them to come soon. Jesus told me that in the spring, when the trees begin to have buds, when all the people begin to believe and they all wear a feather on their heads to show that they believe, He would give back all the dead people. All the people are up there and they are in a hurry to return to you. Now I've told you all this. Try to get more members who will wear a feather on their heads." At that time I believed in it. When I got home, I told people all about it, but they said that it was all lies.

About two weeks later, they[10a] had another one over by Hatchetville. Some missionary who had one wooden leg, came over there. I was there again. The missionary was talking. He said, "What you are doing here is no good. You should take up the Christian way. Someday they are going to take all of you over to the Agency and

[10a] Jim Whitewolf frequently uses a somewhat vague "they," generally meaning the Kiowa Apache people or his own kinsmen. This usage has been left unchanged.

talk to you." After the missionary left that evening, the men began to talk among themselves. The next I heard, this missionary went to Carnegie among the Kiowas. I heard that the Army went over there, too. The Army told them that they wanted this Ghost Dance to stop. They said that it caused a lot of trouble where it started, up north, and that they were going to put a stop to it.[11] But after the Army told them that, they went on and kept having the Ghost Dance.

They called in all the Kiowas who were running the Ghost Dance; they camped by the bridge north of Anadarko. The Agency talked to them. They called in Sam Williams, who always ran the Apache Ghost dances. The agent told all the leaders, "You were warned by the Army not to do this dance. If you do it again, we will put all of you in jail." They didn't have the Ghost Dance after that, as far as I know.

When the fellows who were running the Ghost Dance would give the children a feather to wear, the parents might pay them as much as twenty-five dollars.

WHEN I WAS still pretty small, I remember that east of the Agency near Anadarko, there were some Catholic sisters sitting under an arbor in the camp. Someone was calling out to us to come over there because they had something to tell us. My mother and father took me over there. A fellow was there, named Bill Brownbear, who was interpreting for the Catholic sisters. There was another man with those sisters. This man who was with the sisters prayed, and then there was singing. He took out a black book; it was a Bible. He started reading from it. I didn't understand it at that time. The only thing he was doing that I knew was good was the praying because we had always had praying in the Indian way.[12] Every now and then I could understand a little bit, like when he talked about "our Father," but the rest of the time I didn't know what he was talking about.

---

[11] On the history of efforts to suppress this and other native religious expressions among the Kiowa Apache as well as other Indian groups in Oklahoma, see Charles S. Brant, "Indian-White Cultural Relations in Southwestern Oklahoma," in *The Chronicles of Oklahoma*, 37 : 4 (1959–60), 433–39. James Mooney's classical work *The Ghost Dance Religion and the Sioux Outbreak of 1890*, dealing with the Ghost Dance on a wider basis, is available in paperback reprint (Chicago: Phoenix Books) for readers interested in pursuing the subject further.

[12] That is, prayer was part of traditional Kiowa Apache religious expression; therefore it was perceived as good when performed by a missionary, however different the content of the prayers might be.

When the service was over they said that they would give some of us rosaries. They said that next time they came back they would give out more of them. The men got larger rosaries than the children got. I didn't get any, but my father did. Every two weeks we went to the camp for rations. We went back there again one time—I think it was on Sunday. They had church and went through the same thing as the first time. Then one of the sisters went through the crowd and gave out rosaries. That time I got one. They told me to wear mine all the time. I felt proud of it. I never took it off. I wore it when I slept and even when I went in swimming. People would go back to that service every Sunday, but they went just to get a rosary with beads on the chain. A lot of them didn't even believe in it, but they wanted those beads. I guess those Catholics went around to the Kiowas, too.

The next thing I knew was that the missionary Mr. Methvin was building a church right north of the old Agency. I saw them working on that building. After it was finished, they went around and told people that, when they heard the bell, they should come over there. The people around camp were talking about how this man was going to show them how they could come back after they died. They thought that he was some kind of a medicine man. What he meant was that, if you led a good life, your soul would have eternal life. But the Indians thought that he could bring the dead back to life. Everybody started sending their children to that church. My mother told me that, if I should die, I wouldn't be gone forever but would come back to life. This all happened before I ever went to school.

Another boy and I went to church one time. The preacher was talking and there was a Kiowa fellow alongside him interpreting. Then they divided us up into groups and gave us each a little paper. After that I went to church all the time. Soon some of the older people started to come to church. Later on I began to understand that they meant that when you die you don't return to earth but go up go heaven.

Years after that, I heard that they were going to build another church down by Cache Creek. Then some white people came there. Mr. Curtis came there. Some of us helped haul rocks to build this church. On Sundays Mr. Curtis would come out to where we were camping and talk to us. This was before the church was finished. Bill Brownbear was interpreting for them. Some of the Indians started to believe in it. I guess it was because most of them always had believed in praying.

One time Mr. Curtis said that he was going to read us the Ten Commandments. All I got out of it was the one that says, "Thou shalt not steal." I remembered that one. He said that if you stole you wouldn't go to heaven. Henry Brownbear got up and said, "I used to steal horses, but I don't do it any more." Another old man got up and repeated the commandment, "Thou shalt not lie." He said, "I don't lie. I always tell the truth." Henry Brownbear would get up after every commandment that was read and repeat it. His Indian name was "Old Man Nervous." That was because he had a tremor of the hands. He repeated every single commandment. He was the only one who kept jumping up like that. When Mr. Curtis got to the commandment that said you should not go with another man's wife, Henry Brownbear just whistled and said, "That's too much. I want that woman sitting over there. I guess I'll just have to go to hell." When the reading of the commandments was over, Henry Brownbear got up and told the people that he liked all but that one commandment. When everyone had gone back to camp, he went over to his boy Bill who had been interpreting and told him, "I don't want you to be standing up and telling us all these things. I want you to sit down and not say anything." This was one of my first times in church. I had seen the Catholic services before that, though.

When I was little I stayed with my grandfather. He was a tall, slim man. My grandfather's cousins[13] used to come. They were all old men. My grandfather would bring them over, just one of them at a time, and they would sleep with me and tell me stories. My grandfather told me that the Indians didn't fight among themselves any more. He told me to be friendly to people and never to steal or lie about anything. He said that in the old days the Apaches used to ride from up near the Kansas line down to Mexico, looking for good hunting grounds. Whenever they met up with the Sioux there would be a fight He told me always to get up early in the morning. He said that when I grew up to be a man, always to get up early and feed and water my horses. He said to take care of the horses and keep them fat, because they would take care of me and help me to find

---

[13] All grandparents, grandparents' siblings and grandparents' cousins were addressed by a single kinship term. These relatives commonly acted as mentors and disciplinarians of children.

something to eat. He told me that now I didn't need to have a fast horse to do fighting, but that he wanted me to take care of my horses so I could use them to farm with, like the white people were doing, so I would have something. He said not to forget to plant corn to feed my horses with, and to eat. He said there were many ways to use corn and that there were going to be many more, and that was why I should never forget to raise it. He said that someday I would have a home of my own and I should always have lots of wood to cook food with. At that time they prayed for wood, because it helped to prepare food for them and it kept them warm. He told me always to give blessings for food and to be thankful for my home. He said, "I've told you all these things. Now I am going to tell you some stories. I don't want you to forget them. I want you to remember them so you can tell them to your children and they can tell them to their children." Now I have told you all those old stories, I want you to give them to me so my grandchildren will read them and be able to tell them to their children, too.

WHEN I WAS little, my folks would tell me that if I didn't go to sleep they would call the owl to take me away. One night they told me to go to bed, but I just kept running around. They said, "All right, we are going to sing an owl song. Just watch through the door." I saw something enter the door, something with big eyes. What happened was that my cousin was outside, and he heard them telling me to go to sleep. He took some kind of a pan and painted it like an owl face. That is what I saw in the doorway.[14] I went right to bed. After that, whenever they sang that song, I went right to bed.

[14] Children were sometimes disciplined by frightening them in this manner. The owl was considered by the Kiowa Apache to be an exceedingly dangerous creature. Informants stated that owls were never used for any practical purpose; if killed, they were simply thrown away. It was thought that looking at owls could cause distortion of facial features and bring illness. Owls were conceived as malevolent ghosts of deceased persons, returning to earth to haunt and torment the living. One of the Kiowa Apache ceremonial societies, called *Klintidie*, had an unusual association with the owl. Owl feathers were used in the headdress of the members. During a battle the sound of an owl or the mimicry of one was an irrevocable command to *Klintidie* members to stand their ground regardless of circumstances. When the *Klintidie* society performed its ceremonies, such a sound required that the dancing continue no matter how long it might already have been in progress. One of the *Klintidie* leaders was called *Owl Man*, or, sometimes, *Ghost Man*. See Introduction, pp. 9–10.

Sometimes my folks would call in my cousin when I wouldn't mind. He would take me down to the creek and throw me in whether it was cold or not. After this happened to me, I always knew that was what they would do, so I behaved.

Sometimes I talked dirty[15] at home. When you were around your sisters, you weren't supposed to talk nasty. My mother was telling an old lady that I sure talked dirty sometimes. I talked that way when my mother's brother was around. One time my uncle was there, and I talked nasty. My mother went out and spoke to the old lady. This old lady got a sharp piece of glass and came over. She told me that she knew I was always talking dirty. She grabbed me and threw me down on my back. She cut my lip with the glass until it bled. Then she asked if I was going to talk that way anymore, and I said I wouldn't. They did that to a lot of kids who talked dirty.

When I was small, I learned about how babies were born by listening to old women who talked about it. They never were ashamed to talk about those things in front of a small boy. It was only after you got older that they wouldn't talk like that in front of you.

When I was a little boy and my grandfather came and stayed with me, he taught me many things. He said that when I grew up and got married I should always consider my mother before my wife. A wife might leave you or cause you trouble. He told me, "Grandson, you can always get another wife if your wife dies or leaves you, but you can't ever get another mother."

He told me how to get a wife. He said that you could tell by a girl's facial expression when you talked with her if she liked you. My grandfather taught me that there were two ways. You could run away with a girl, or you could get somebody to go and talk to her folks for you. She would do what her father and her brother wanted her to do. Maybe, if her folks didn't like you, they would send word back that they couldn't decide for their daughter whom she would marry. That is just what they would say if they didn't want you to marry their daughter.

My grandfather taught me that when I got married I should treat my wife's father and mother well and do things for them.[16] He said

15 "Dirty talk" here means sexual talk.
16 Matrilocality, bringing a man into a relationship of obligation and respect towards his parents-in-law, was the most common form of residence but it was not obligatory.

that if I treated them well they would help me if I had trouble with my wife. If my wife died, they would give me another one of their daughters.

WHEN I WAS a pretty small boy, my grandmother used to tell me, "Always wear your moccasins when you walk around. Don't run around with your hair blowing everywhere." She braided my hair for me. My mother told her to raise me right and take care of me.

I had two dogs that I played with. My grandfather fixed a rope for me to lasso the dogs with and lead them around by. He made me a set of arrows and a bow. The arrows were blunt-ended and the bow was small, like children used. He told me not to shoot at anything except birds.[17] He told me, "Certain boys go way off when they play. Don't go with them because they are crazy."[18] He said to swim only with boys my own size, because big boys might drown me. I would play around with my bow and arrow until I got tired of it; then I would rope my dogs and pretend they were horses. When my father went out to round up his horses I rode with him, on the back of the saddle. He showed me how to stop a horse to catch it. I would hold out my hand like I was going to feed him and then he would stop. I learned how to hobble horses, too.

My grandfather used to get me up early. Before that I sometimes slept late. He would say, "Get up! Wash your face and comb your hair."

One time he caught one of his gentlest horses and told me, "Ride him bareback." In the evening I rode that horse as we took the other horses to be watered. That is how he taught me to ride. When I had learned, he pointed out a certain boy who liked to hunt. He told me, "Go with him to chase rabbits and shoot birds." Sometimes we brought in rabbits to eat.

One morning my grandfather got me up early and said, "Take your horse. Put the bridle on him and go out and water our horses. Take off the hobbles and put the ropes around their necks. Take

17 Small boys were expected not to kill any animals. Practicing with blunt arrows by shooting at birds was considered a way for them to achieve marksmanship.

18 That is, careless and irresponsible, and not likely to protect a small boy against the danger of getting lost.

them down to the water. You have seen how I do it." I did it myself that time.

As I went around with other boys chasing rabbits and squirrels, some of us got to be pretty good shots with a bow and arrow. Later I was taught to shoot a .44 Winchester. My grandfather took me out by a hill and put down a bone for a target. He showed me how to sight with the rifle. At first I was a little afraid. I didn't shoot very well at the beginning; the bullets just went off anywhere. My grandfather never let me have the rifle; he always kept it. He explained to me how to sight with the rifle. By this time I was growing up to be a pretty good-sized boy.

Then my grandfather gave me a rope, a bridle and saddle. He said I knew how to handle horses and could go about it myself. The saddle had a case on it for the rifle. Then he gave me the rifle.

Sometime before the country opened up[19] my grandfather died. They didn't kill his horse at the funeral or anything like that in the old-time way. My father said to me, "Now that your grandfather is gone, some of these horses will be yours. Take care of them as he taught you to." My grandfather, before he died, had told my father which of the horses were to be mine.

I went home to stay with my father and mother then. They made a place for me to sleep. They made me buckskin clothes to wear when I went to the dances. I had a buckskin jacket that went on over my head, and leggings that fitted tight. My father told me, "You have horses, clothes, saddle and bridle. You have your own things, so when you get married you are all ready." That is how they raised kids those days. They said that if you had a good start and were raised up right you would be a well-respected man when you grew up.

Now I have tried to teach my own grandson Willy some of the things I learned from my grandfather. I have already shown him different kinds of seeds and what they are for. Later on I will teach him more things.

When I was very small I played around sometimes with little girls. We chased each other around and went in swimming. Later on my grandmother and other old women got stingy and would not allow

---

[19] That is, prior to extensive white settlement and individual allotment of the tribal reservation.

the girls to play with us boys. They would say to the girls, "See that boy? He is getting big now. Don't play with him any more; he might do something to you." That is the way they taught girls. But sometimes a grandmother wouldn't care. Those girls would get played around with by the boys.

That is how they raised you up in the old days. They gave you things and taught you things, and when you were grown they would tell you, "Use these things right. Do not cheat or lie. Treat others right and do not hurt their feelings." They said that if you did not act right, others would laugh at you, and everything you had would be poor. Then you would be ashamed. They said, "When you get married and have your children, raise them in a religious way." Up to the time I got married I did the things I was told.

When I was growing up I saw something of how my grandmother taught my sister. She showed her how to make little tipis out of cloth and how to make little cradles. She told her to keep the little tipis clean. As girls grew older they were taught how to make bigger tipis and how to cook. They would ask for a piece of the meat when the women were cooking, and take it to their own fires and put it in a bucket, just like they saw the women do. When my sister was grown up, my mother's half-sister taught her to do beadwork. My sister watched her and tried to imitate her as she sewed and made baby clothes. Her playdays were over now. She watched my mother and learned how to cook and to prepare meals. After she went to school she began to sew her own clothes at home. When she got married she had all her own things.

THIS IS about the food we ate when I was young.

They used to slice the meat up thin and hang it up to dry in the sun. That way it would keep for the winter. My mother used to put it into a bag made of hide to keep it. She broke up the bones of the cow and boiled them to get the grease out. She put the grease into a bag of cow udder that had a buckskin drawstring. She didn't like buckets because she thought they would spoil things. The meat from the back of the animal she cooked and dried. It was something like bacon. She took the large intestine and stuffed it with a long piece of meat, raw. The whole thing was boiled and eaten.

We gathered wild grapes in the fall. They were boiled up, mixed with a little flour, and made into balls like hamburgers. They put them into a skin bag to keep. There were wild blue grapes, with seeds in them. It used to be women's work to gather the grapes, but when I was young, boys did it too. Wild plums were prepared in the same way.

Mesquite beans were ground up sometimes with rocks and put away. Some people just kept them as they were. They used the ground-up ones like cornmeal.

Hackberries grew on big trees. They were ground up and formed into balls and put away. There was another berry that we call "rock sour." They were dried and kept too.

When I was a boy, living with my parents, we had dried meat and dried fruit for every meal. We used to have meat soup a lot too. We ate eggs from wild turkeys and prairie chickens, boiled hard. Whenever we ate fish, they were cooked right in the ashes. Rabbits were roasted that way too.

My favorite food was ground-up meat with sugar mixed in it. They mixed the meat with marrow before they sweetened it. All the small children like this the best. My mother would give it to me all the time. They used the meat from the backbone to make pounded meat for the children. They kept it separate from the other meat. People who had a lot of pounded meat on hand were considered well off. It was kept for times when there wasn't much fresh meat to be gotten.

My father's sister[20] always treated me good. When I went there she would feed me well. She would make me a good bed to sleep in, and sometimes she sewed my clothes and shoes. Whenever I went to see my grandmother, she gave my mother dried fruits to give me. My mother's brother's wife[20] would do the same.

WHEN I WAS a small boy, there were only antelopes, deer and wild turkeys. I don't remember any buffalo.

[20] A child called his father's sister by the same kinship term as he used for stepfather. His relations with her were restrained and respectful, as with a step-father, but lacked the element of fear. With mother's brother's wife, relations were less formal, and she tended to be preferred by the child, as against his father's sister. A child was on terms of greater familiarity and intimacy with his mother's brother than with any other relative in his parents' generation. This was a warm, close relationship, characterized by joking and teasing, sometimes ribald in nature, and by great indulgence on the uncle's part.

One time they were gathering together to talk about hunting. They wanted only the fastest horses, the ones that knew how to follow the deer. I had a small pony then. Some old Kiowas gave it to my mother and she gave it to me. I never had gone out with it chasing deer or antelopes. I just went out on the prairies with it to chase coyotes. That morning, just east of where Apache Joe's home now is, they were going to gather together early. They started from there and when they got up north of what is now Apache, they scattered out. Some went up on high ground and some went down into low places. Just east of where I was riding, someone hollered and they began to shoot. Then I saw three deer come out into an open place. They began to chase these deer all around, and then the horses got tired and these fellows started to fall back. One deer came rushing towards me and I ran right into it with my horse. It knocked the deer down as I jumped from my horse. I ran over where the deer was lying and grabbed hold of it. A big fellow rode up and cut the deer's throat with a knife. Then he grabbed a hind leg and said, "This is going to be mine." The others rode up and jumped off their horses. There were six parts of the deer, the four legs and the sides. Each of the six men claimed a part and I was left with just the backbone and the hide. They washed the kidneys, liver and the gall in blood and ate them right there. They took a piece of the gall and put it on the liver, to give it a salty, bitter taste. When they were through butchering and each had his share, they went back. That was the law about hunting deer. The one that killed it got only the backbone and the hide. On the way back one of the fellows with a Winchester .44 shot two more deer we saw. Then two fellows had a race to the deer to claim their parts. I got a part, the ribs. We went on back to camp. That was the first time I ever went deer hunting.

The next time I went hunting it was near Alden, south of Carnegie. There were four of us. We got four elks. One of the men said, "Today we will break the rule. We will each take a whole one." But the others said "No" and so they raced for the animals and took what each could grab. I managed to get three legs. That hunt was in the summertime.

THE FIRST TIME I heard of them giving us rations up in Anadarko was just before we went on the elk hunt. They had been giving rations before but this was the first time I was going to get rations. My family had a ticket which said how many there were in the family. We camped in Anadarko and my mother and father went to get our rations. This was northeast of Anadarko, where they had a long building in which they kept the rations. The Kiowas, Comanches and Apaches were all camping in that area, some right near the fairgrounds.

When they issued out the things they never cared about the size, so we would pass things around the family to see if the things fitted anybody. People were going all over the camp trading things back and forth, to find the right size. You always would find the right fit somewhere. The first time I saw my grandfather get rationed they gave him some pants and told him what they were for. He said "No" and cut the pants off at the thighs. He put on the two legs and threw the rest away. Then he put his breech cloth on around his waist. When they gave us shoes all the old people would cut off the heels and throw them away. They said the heels were no good to them.[21]

The people who had already been given their allotments and who wanted to work were given wire for fencing, wagons, harnesses and plows. My grandfather was issued a big, heavy wagon with a box on it for hauling grain. He said that it was too heavy to haul around, so he threw it away. He went down into the timber and cut some willows and made himself a smaller, lighter box.

This was at the time we were given other rations, like bacon and rice. We got dried fruit too. Some of it they just threw away. They said the bacon came from way off east, where there were big fat water snakes. They said if you ate the rice it would give you worms. That was why they threw those two things away. I never heard of the agent saying anything about us throwing the stuff away, but he knew about it. We had Indian police[22] in the camp to watch out for people stealing things. There were police all around this territory then, watching to see that the white people didn't steal the timber or anything. All of this I saw with my own eyes.

MY MOTHER was a short, stout woman. As far back as I can remember her, she told me not to run around and get mixed up with kids

---

[21] Moccasins, the traditional footwear, were flat.

[22] Indians appointed by the local administrators of Indian affairs of the federal government.

that did wrong. I used to stay pretty close by her. When I was a little older, she used to take me down to the creek. There were always a lot of other children there with their mothers. In those days the women folks used to go to get the wood. The children would all swim while their mothers gathered the wood. We would get out of the creek when the women were through cutting the wood; they would go down where we had been swimming and take sticks and cover up our tracks. The oldest woman in the group would call back towards the creek where we had been swimming. She would call the names of all the children who had been swimming there. She would call, "You had better all go home. We are going home." After that, every time my mother and I would go to the creek, she would do like that. She would call, "You better go home. We are going." The reason they covered up all the children's tracks was that they were afraid that ghosts[23] would come around at night and follow the children's tracks, causing them to get sick. The reason the women would call back toward the creek like that was to call all the voices of the children to them, to take home. That way, the ghosts couldn't get hold of the children's voices and make them sick. After I grew up a little, my mother got two dry walnuts and bored holes through them. She took a strip of buckskin and put it through the nuts and tied it around my wrist. She did it to both wrists. They believed then that it would protect me against ghosts if I went around at night. That is the reason my mother kept me close to her. She wanted me to learn all these things. She told me that I wouldn't get ghost-sickness after she tied those walnuts to my wrists. Another thing I remember was that, before I would leave home at night to go around to the hand games,[23a] she would take ashes and put a cross of ashes on my forehead and on my chest to protect me. These are the things my parents believed in and what they did for me. Other parents believed in different things and did them for their sons.

One time a whirlwind was coming up. When it came toward me, my parents covered me up. When it got past, they took the blanket off me. My folks told me, "The reason we did this is that your eyes might get crossed and you might get sick if you are not covered up."

[23] The Kiowa Apache, like all Apache tribes, had a lively fear of ghosts of the dead. These were believed to be able to return to haunt the living, cause sickness and disaster. Young children were considered especially vulnerable.

[23a] See p. 114 ff. for description of the hand game.

When I had grown up, my mother told me, "Don't forget all these things I have taught you. When you are married and have children, teach your children the same way." I went around by myself after that.

She told me other things. She told me, when I was getting married, "When your wife is pregnant, don't lie in bed late." I asked her why she wanted me to do this. She explained to me that if I stayed late in bed, my wife would have a difficult time giving birth. She told me that, when my wife was going to have a child, I should untie my shoestrings and unbutton my shirt so that she would have an easy time giving birth to the child. She said that the child's diaper should never be put on the ground or on the floor because the dogs could urinate on it. That would make the child sick, she told me. My mother told me to tell my wife that if she ever had to leave a child alone, she should lay a piece of grass or a stick on the child. In that way the ghosts would not bother it.

IT WAS WHEN I was about seven or eight years old that I heard about the Rabbit Dance (Kasowe), but I never went around there. I was kind of scared of it. One day I was playing around the camp in Anadarko, and I heard that they were going to have this dance. Frank Allen's brother and Jack Smokey's brother and I were going to go to it. When we got there, all the kids were there. There was a tipi with the sides up above the ground, and the people standing around outside could see the kids dancing inside. We all went inside. All the kids had their own bowls to eat out of. Everyone was sitting down in there. The man inside who was in charge of the dance was talking to them.

Some of the boys were bigger. None of these kids had ever taken part in any kind of dance. The Rabbit Dance was their first dance. The man in charge stuck a big knife in the ground in front of him and said, "Those of you who don't dance will get your hair cut off or some of your clothing cut off." He picked out one of the biggest boys who was dancing and told him, "You are in charge. Those that don't dance, use the whip on them. Take the knife and cut some of their hair off." The whip was flat and made of wood. The man took his drum and started singing. The big boy in charge told us all to get up and dance. He told us to put our hands up by the sides of our heads like rabbit ears. Everybody was dancing. We were afraid that the fellow in charge would whip us or cut our hair if we didn't do it. The man sang four songs and we danced; then we stopped. Then he prayed. He was praying for all of us children. After he prayed, he picked out two boys who dished out the food that was outside the tipi. After we were through eating, the dance was all over. This dance was in the morning. It was kind of a church. It was like having a prayer meeting for a sick child. They would have these dances for children when they reached a certain age. This dance was being held for a boy who had been sick and gotten well. *Kasowe* just means "rabbit."

The last Rabbit Dance they ever had was just before the First World War, about 1915. It was being given by Susie Williams for her boy. Apache John was in charge of it. Big Alex was chosen to take the whip. At that time it was the belief that someone who had a medicine bundle [24] should be in charge. Apache John told Big Alex, "Take this knife and whip. If any of them don't dance, whip them and cut their hair and clothing." Apache John took his drum and began to sing. He told them all to dance like rabbits. I remember that Big Ben was outside the tipi. He said that he was going to visit and eat when they finished dancing. I was holding a baby of mine. I danced. Big Alex was a pretty tough fellow. He went outside and told all the adults watching out there to dance or they would get the same punishment as the children on the inside. When the dancing was over, there was prayer, and then everyone ate. My wife, Louisa, was with me, and she got her sleeves cut for not dancing. This was the last Rabbit Dance I ever saw.

I WAS ABOUT nine or ten years old. Some old man was talking one morning in camp. He said, "Take the kids all down to the creek to swim. Last night I had a dream that some bad sickness is coming. Have them all swim. Then they won't get the sickness." All the little kids had paint in their hands. When they got out into the water, they dropped the paint. It was red clay paint.

All the people went to the creek early that morning. The parents built a big, long fire. When they took the kids to the creek, it was so cold that you could see ice floating on top of the water. They were all wearing blankets. When the praying was over, we jumped into the water and turned the paint loose. Then we came back by the fire.

[24] See pp. 7–8.

The paint was to protect us against the sickness. When I came up out of the water, I could hardly breathe. When we got back up on the hill, we got dressed and went back to our camps. That was the belief in the old days. When a medicine man dreamed, we had to follow it. I swam because that medicine man had a dream.

I HAD a brother, born after me. Then there was another brother, and then my sister. The brother next to me they called Billy Spotted Horse. My next younger brother died very young and didn't have a name.[24a] My sister's name meant Sunshine Cloud. The Agency called her Patsy, but she was known as Patricia. My brother was a better boy than I was. We went around together when we were small, and I was the one who would get mad. My brother never got mad at me.[25] I was older than my brother, but he went to school before I did. He started young. I was still running around. I was the pet. The old Apaches always said that the oldest one was respected the most. My brother went to the Kiowa School, and later he went to the mission school west of Apache. It was then that I started to school at the Kiowa School.

Later on my sister started to school over at the mission. The mission people liked my brother, and they would always take him along when they went around making visits to the people. The white women in those days would ride sidesaddle. He would interpret for them when they went around to the camps. When my brother would come home, he would tell my folks what he had learned. It was my brother who got my folks to be baptized at the Presbyterian Church over at Cache Creek. I was the oldest, but I never did tell my folks about the things I was learning. My brother would work at the Presbyterian Church when school was out in the summer. Later on, my sister was baptized at that church. I wasn't baptized. I just ran around here and there and never went to church. When the older people began to die off and after my brother died, there was no one there to interpret, and so my folks changed to the Baptist Church. My brother died a young boy. Mr. Carithers told us to get a tombstone for my brother's grave. My mother gave Mr. Carithers some money, and

[24a] See footnote 3, above.

[25] Being even-tempered, avoiding angry behavior, was an important Kiowa Apache value; hence the equation of "never got mad" with being a "better boy."

he bought a tombstone.[26] I think that my brother was the first Apache to have a tombstone. That is all that I remember of my brother.

My sister lived until 1927. She was married to Henry Moon. She was his second wife. I never went around with my sister when she was young. She went with the girls. That was the Apache way. My sister was good at sewing. She made cradles with beads on them. My sister always treated me well. She would do things for me. But I never talked close to her. Brother and sister are kind of ashamed. That is the Apache way.[27] My sister and my brother were good. I was always kind of crazy. I never cheated or stole, but I wanted to drink and run around with women. That is what busted me up. I think that my brother and sister liked my mother better than my father. But I liked my father. I liked the way my father gambled and ran around with women, and I did just like he did. He was a bad one. Before he was a scout, he left from Kansas and went down to Mexico and stayed around for five years. He stole horses, gambled and fought down there.

BEFORE the country opened up, back about 1885, we got grass-lease money from the government. It was about nine dollars a head. Three years or so later, we heard that the government was going to issue cattle to every Indian. We were told to come to Anadarko for the cattle issue. I was small then, so my father went to get our cattle. All the tribes around here got them, too. Then, a little before the country opened up, they issued out some more cattle. The government gave each family a different brand so that they could mark their own cattle. We put our brand on our horses and also on all new-born calves. Herds would get mixed up; that is why they put the brands on them. Before they issued my cattle, I got a paper. A man called out my name, looked at my paper, and then branded some cattle and drove them into a corral. When they did that with everyone, we drove all the cattle homeward and then separated them out. We raised those cattle and marketed some of them on the hoof in Anadarko. Some of them we milked.

---

[26] Grave markers were probably introduced through white contact. In aboriginal times the Kiowa Apache buried their dead hastily, did not mark graves and avoided them sedulously.

[27] Restraint, amounting almost to avoidance, characterized brother-sister relations after puberty, in the aboriginal culture.

When we were first issued cattle, nobody knew how to milk them. Only those who had been to school knew anything about milking. Over where Frank Allen now lives they had a corral of cattle. We didn't know how to milk them. One of the boys roped a cow and tied her head to a post in the middle of the corral. They tied up her hind legs so she wouldn't kick. They did that to several of them. Two boys knew how to milk, and they were going to show the rest of us. They had learned it in school. One of them started milking. He asked one of the boys to try it. He grabbed hold of the teats and started squeezing them. Nothing came out. I tried it, and nothing came out. I squeezed and twisted and pulled, but nothing came out at all. The two boys who knew how went ahead and milked, and we just watched them. They took the milk home. I took some too. I had never drunk milk much before that. I didn't like it. There was an old Mexican and his wife living near us. He asked me to give him the milk. Later on, all of us who had cattle tried to learn to milk, but I never did become very good at it.

When the white people started coming in, the pasture and grazing lands got smaller. That's why the Indians got rid of their herds of cattle and horses. Before that, the herds grazed around freely everywhere.

I don't remember that many of us tried to go into the towns and get jobs after the country opened up. Some of us cut blocks of wood and sold them to people in the towns who used them as foundations for houses.

It was in 1893 that I first heard the expression "Fourth of July." I heard that in Anadarko there was going to be a big celebration. There was a race track by the old Agency. There were four posts on the track with ropes hanging down with rings on them. You were supposed to ride past and thrust a stick into the rings. If you made all four, you got twenty-five dollars. If you made two, you got twelve dollars. There were horse races, too. There were three prizes for horse racing. They had foot racing for small boys. Before this time, I remember only going to dances, but this was called "Fourth of July celebration."

They had a group contest among six tribes—Kiowas, Kiowa Apaches, Comanche, Caddo, Wichita and Delaware. We were supposed to dress up in the Indian way. The best group got prizes of

food, and there was money in it too. Each group had a white man
in charge. The morning of the contest we all dressed up. We paraded
around. The judges came over and rode among us. The Apache
group won. Afterward we went to the race track. They had the races.
Alonzo Redbird beat all the kids in the foot races. That was my
first Fourth of July celebration. We were given free lemonade, and
there was free beef distributed to us too.

THE FIRST TIME that I was ever taken to a medicine man was when
I was pretty small. My mother told me about it years later when I was
older. She said that I was pretty sick once. The medicine man who
cured me told her never to feed me dog meat. At that time, my people
ate small dogs. My mother told me that I had better not eat any dog
meat, ever. I never have. Recently I was up in South Dakota where
the Sioux were having a Sun Dance. I went there with Fred Kills-
first. I was a visitor, and they told me to sit on the north side by the
chief. This was the last day of the dance. They were going to have a
big dinner in the arbor after the dance ended. Four boys were carrying
pans of food around for the people. I saw that there was dog meat
there. I recognized the feet and legs. As soon as I saw it, I remembered
what my mother told me a long time ago about eating dog meat.
I didn't know what to do. I felt as if I was in a trap. I was a visitor.
They came around to me with the meat, and one of the boys
explained that the dog meat was just for the ten men who were the
chiefs of the Sun Dance. He said that they were going to serve the
rest of the people with beef, elk, deer, antelope and buffalo meat. The
government had given it to them. I had deer meat. I was glad that
it was that way. If they had said that I should take dog meat, I don't
know what I would have done because I was afraid of it. I wouldn't
want to go against their ways either.

SOMETIME before I went to school, I went on a turkey chase. We
camped over near where Harry Sunchild now lives. Logan's father
and my father were cousins. That is why he liked me. One afternoon
he started home. When he came back, he said that he had seen a lot
of turkeys running around in the green grass. It was springtime. He
wanted to chase them. I didn't have a horse. Logan said that I
could ride behind him on his horse. We rode northward toward the

creek. Soon we saw a lot of turkeys. They started flying off. A big
gobbler was running by the creek, and then he went into a white
man's pasture nearby. Logan told me to get off and chase it. I
handed Logan my moccasins. I could run better barefooted. I
caught up to the turkey and tried to grab him, but he got away. I fell
down. I chased him, and he got away about three or four times. The
turkey jumped across a ditch, and I went over after him. I grabbed
him and fell down and held on to him. I was tired. Logan came up.
He saw blood on my right big toe. It was twisted. Logan cut a piece
off of his wristlet and tied up my toe. I didn't feel much pain. I rode
back to camp with Logan. Then it began to feel heavy and hurt me.
My father and another man carried me into the tipi. There were no
white doctors around there. It hurt all that night. I couldn't sleep.
Next day it was all swollen. I was crying too. An old lady came over.
It was my mother's aunt. She told my mother, "I have a good
medicine. It was made a long time ago. My grandfather gave it to
me. Put up a tipi over there and make a fire. This boy and I will
stay there four nights. That is the way my grandfather told me to do.
No one else can come in. Bring us food and water." When the tipi
was up, they fixed a place for the old lady to sleep on the north side
and a place for me on the south side. The old lady went out and came
back with some white roots. It is called "pain medicine." She
pounded up the root outside the tipi. She untied the bandage on my
toe. She chewed some of the root and then rubbed it on my toe.
Then she put some of it in the fire, and smoke came up. She took a
piece of hide and held it over the fire to warm. Then she put it on
my toe. She prayed as she did it. She prayed to the power that had
given her grandfather the medicine. In her prayer she said, "You
are the power that gave this medicine a long time ago. Now it has
come to me. I am going to use it to help this boy get well. Help me."
She kept warming the hide and putting it on my toe.

The next morning I woke up, and the fire was already going. She
called me "grandson." You know that was the way; any old woman
would call a young boy "grandson." She asked how I felt. I said
that the pain was not so bad now. She said that she would treat me
some more after I had eaten. She had to bring me a bucket so I
could go to the toilet because I couldn't walk. Then she prayed and
put the warm buckskin on my toe again. After we had eaten dinner,
she sat down and said, "Grandson, this medicine isn't mine. It has

come to me from a long time back. My grandfather learned this medicine for curing broken bones."

In the evening she told me a story about her young days, and I fell asleep while she was talking.

She treated me like this for four days. On the fourth day, my mother and father came in. My swelling was gone, and I was all right again.

I don't know where that medicine is now. Maybe Mary Allen has it now because it was her grandmother who doctored me. I don't think they use medicines like that any more; the young fellows don't believe in it any more. But in those days the old people never believed in the white man's medicine. They believed in their own ways.

II

Stories of Our People

Now I am going to tell you some things I heard about.

At the time of the treaty of Medicine Lodge, up in Kansas, they asked the Kiowas, Comanches and Apaches where they wanted to settle. The three tribes wanted to come down here, where they are now. The Cheyennes wanted to just roam and not settle down any-where at all. The Arapaho came down here, with the Kiowa, Comanche and Apache. Then the Arapaho got the Cheyennes to come down this way and settle. The Apaches settled by Mount Scott. The Kiowas, Comanches and some other tribe that I don't remember camped near the Agency at Anadarko. The soldiers always camped north of Anadarko, near the Riverside Indian School. Later the Apaches moved up near Verden. We had to stay within certain boundaries then. Before that we used to go out and fight the white people, but now they had put boundaries around us. The Kiowas and Comanches at this time would go down to Texas and Mexico raiding for horses and cattle, and the government kept telling them they had to stop it. Before Medicine Lodge the Apaches used to go on those raids, but after the treaty the Apaches never took part. The Army told our chief, Peso, not to go on the raids. He told our people and so they never did go. Peso was a good leader. We began to lead a better life.

When we were at Verden we heard that there was trouble at the Agency where other tribes were camping. Soldiers came in and started fighting the Indians in the camp and scattered them everywhere. Peso picked out some men and sent them down to find out what the trouble was about. He told them to put a white cloth on a stick and carry it, so nobody would bother them. The fellow who was carrying the stick could speak Mexican. They could see the soldiers all en-camped north of Anadarko, right by the river. The soldiers watched them coming in, carrying the white flag, and they didn't shoot at them. The fellow who was carrying the flag spoke out in Mexican

65

and told the soldiers, "We came down to find out what this trouble is all about. Our chief sent us down. We are camping east of here. We don't want any part in this. If you will give us permission, we want to go over to Fort Sill. We want to get along, without any trouble." The officer in charge, who had braid and epaulets on his shoulders, gave them a paper and a flag to carry. It was an American flag. He told them to break their camp and to carry this flag on their journey to Fort Sill. He said that if they carried an American flag no one would bother them.

As the Apaches approached Fort Sill carrying the flag they were spotted from atop the hill by the soldiers who were using field glasses. They sent out a soldier to meet them. The Apaches gave him the paper. The soldiers showed us a place west of where the old fort was located, and said we could camp there. There were a few Kiowas camping there too. At that time Kicking Bird was chief of the Kiowas. Quanah Parker brought some of the Comanches there to stay, too. We ate well over there; they gave us lots of meat and treated us good. The told us to stay right in that area and not to go far off, because they were going to be watching us.

There was one day at Fort Sill when the head man of the Army called in Peso, Quanah Parker and Kicking Bird. He told the Apache chief to choose three men who knew the country well and could travel with the Army and be depended upon. They wanted them to go out to bring in scattered Indians to the Fort Sill encampments. He asked the Kiowa and Comanche chiefs to do the same thing.

Peso went back to the camp and announced to everyone that he wanted all the men to gather at his camp. He explained what the Army wanted. He said, "We all know each other and we know who are the best men. Go ahead and pick out your three men." The men talked it over and chose my father, Soontay and Nokozis. After these men were chosen they were asked if they would work for the Army and they agreed. I don't know who the Kiowas and the Comanches chose. These men got soldier's clothing and started working for the Army. They would send these scouts out to cover certain territories every day.

One day they sent my father out to Saddle Mountain to look out for some Indians. They said that the soldiers with wagons would be following my father, with an Apache scout along with them. One of the soldiers told my father that they were going to camp at a certain place near Saddle Mountain. They told him that if he spotted any Indians he should not ride into their camp but return to the soldier party and tell them the location. Night came upon my father near Saddle Mountain and he stayed there overnight by himself. Early in the morning he got his horse saddled up and rode along the creek. North of him he heard shots. When he looked he saw a lot of people who looked as if they were moving a camp. When he saw these people he got off his horse and tied everything he had with him to the saddle so that if he were chased he wouldn't lose anything. He stopped and remembered what the soldiers had told him, to ride back immediately if he saw anyone. But he saw they were Kiowas and some of his relatives were among them. His mother was a Kiowa. These relatives recognized him. They were coming close to him and he rode right up to them. Four of them approached him. He looked at them and they greeted him. They called him "Son." Some of them called him "Brother." They asked where the soldiers were and he told them they were east of there. They all looked pitiful. Their hair was all undone, their horses looked in bad shape, and some of these people were on foot. They were all hungry. My father had some hardtack and some hard sugar in his saddlebag and he divided it among the children, who looked very bad. The leader of the group asked my father what the Army was going to do to them, whether the Army was going to kill them off. My father told them that if they went down to Fort Sill they would be fed and treated all right. He said he would ride back to where the soldiers were and tell them to come after these Kiowas with the wagons and take them back. My father was on the way back to the Army camp when he saw a horse, all alone, tied up. This was kind of a bait the Army used then; if Indians saw a stray horse they might go for it, and soldiers would be lying in wait hiding. For some reason my father fired a shot into the air, even though the Army had taught him never to fire. All of a sudden the soldiers came riding up. A soldier who spoke Comanche asked him where he had seen Indians. My father told him there were some further west. My father changed horses and led the soldiers over to where the Kiowas were. As the soldiers approached they were getting food ready to feed these people. My father took some of the soldiers over to lead the Indians back on foot, while the rest of the soldiers prepared the food for them. They spread out a long table and fed the Indians. They fed them meat and beans. At night the soldiers gave them blankets to sleep on. The soldiers formed a circle around them to guard them during the night. In the morning the Indians were fed again, and those on foot were put into the wagons, while the ones with horses rode. There were no roads at that time; they just rode over the prairie.

As they were riding along, a certain woman would ride up close alongside of my father. She did this several times. Another Apache scout asked my father if he knew this woman. He told my father that she was Apache Joe's sister. She was married to a Kiowa. This scout told my father, "Next time she rides up, just as she gets close to us, I will call her name." My father and the other scout rode along and were talking as she came up again. He called, "Hey, is that you?" and called her name. She said, "Yes, that is me." I don't remember what her name was. My father and the scout told her to ride along right where she was and that they would go up ahead and ask the officers if they could take her back to the Apache camp because she was an Apache woman. The Army officer told them that when they reached a camping place for the night they should bring her over where they were unhitching their horses.

When my father and the other scout got to the camping place they fixed a place where they would sleep for the night, apart from the other soldiers. Then this woman came over to them. The officer came over and said, "We will find out if she is really an Apache. There's a bucket over there. Tell her in Apache to get it and bring over some water. If she is really an Apache she will understand and do it." The other scout gave her this order in Apache. She took the bucket, went to the creek, and brought it back full of water. The officer said they had proved she was Apache, so he would send her back to the Apaches. He said they should fix her a bed close to them, so she could eat and sleep near them, and that the next day when they approached the Apache camp my father and the other scout could take her over to it.

By noon the next day they reached Fort Sill and showed her where the Apaches were camping. Before they reached the camp these Indians and soldiers ran into another group of soldiers. This group asked where the Indians were being taken. They said not to take them back to Fort Sill but to take them out somewhere and kill them off. The soldiers who were escorting these Indians to Fort Sill

said, "No, we found these people and they all look poor and pitiful."
The soldier group then agreed to let them be taken on to Fort Sill
and be taken care of.

When they finally got to the fort, they gathered together by the
flagpole with four officers. The men all stayed there and the women
went in the wagons over to a place by the railroad track. After all
these people got settled down there, they were issued clothing, food,
utensils and tents.

Right next to where the highway now is there was a big jail, and
they threw all the men into jail. That night the officers called a
meeting of the Kiowa, Apache and Comanche chiefs. They told
Kicking Bird, the Kiowa chief, to call out all the men of his group
that had been making trouble. These men and the Kiowa captives
who were Mexicans were going to be sent off to prison. The officers
wanted to know which ones were Kiowas and which ones were
Mexicans. The next day they took the ones who were really mean and
put them in a dungeon. The officers and the three tribal chiefs got
together to talk over what should be done with these men. Quanah
Parker said that these men had families and small children, and that
the Army should find a place for them to live and warn them to
behave. He said that if they did wrong again, the Army should find
the troublemakers and send them off.

The following day the scouts from the three tribes were given
permission to go down to the dungeon. They called out the men who
had been making the trouble and told them to go back to their
families and stay there until they were told what to do. Every day
the scouts went down to the dungeon and called out a few of these
men and sent them back to their families. After all the Kiowas had
been sent back to their families, the Mexican captives were the only
ones left. They were sentenced to five years in prison and sent off
east somewhere. The Kiowa leaders were given life imprisonment and
sent to Texas.

That is all of this story. After my father saw that all the Indians
that were scattered out had been rounded up, he and the other scouts
quit. My father got a pension from the Army. He was an old man
by that time.

BEFORE I WENT to school, the older people used to tell a story
about where our people came from. It was then that I heard this

story. It is not my story, but it belongs to five fellows who told it to me.

A long time ago, the Kiowa Apache were north of here. It was wild country, somewhere around where the Crow Indians lived. There were no horses yet. We moved around with dogs. This was a very long time ago. Knives were made of rock and clothing of buffalo hides.

Then they began moving this way. They were in North Dakota. Then they came down into South Dakota. They were there for a long time. There were many tribes around there, moving about, and every once in a while we got into a fight with them. The Apaches then moved farther down this way. For a while they were around a river called Shell River. Then they moved down toward Kansas. They came to what they called the Iron River.[1] I don't know why they called it that. While we were near that river, it was the first time the white people gave us anything. They gave us food and clothing. They gave us things in the fall to use during the winter. They stayed around there for a long time.

The next time they moved, they came down here by Mount Scott. We were rationed from Fort Sill. They were there a few years and then moved to Anadarko. When we came into this area here, we were just scattered out.

It is said that we met the Kiowas around the Black Hills. We kept coming south together with them. Sometimes they camped in a different place from the Apaches. But as far as I know, the two tribes have always stayed together. While the Kiowas and our people were coming southward, we met up with the Arapaho. We never had any trouble with them.

WHEN MY father used to go to the Southwest and Mexico he would meet up with wagon trains of white people going west. There would always be one man in the front of the wagon train on horseback.

One time when they met up with a wagon train, the Indians got ahead of it. Some of them dismounted and hid by the roadside. The rest of them, with faster horses, went further ahead. When the wagon train approached the men who were hiding, they planned

[1] Probably in northwestern Wisconsin.

to attack it, and if the whites should run, the Indians with the faster horses would go after them.

As the wagon-train leader passed by the hidden men, he was shot at by the last man he passed. He was hit and turned back. Then the first two that he had passed rode up as he fell. One of them hit him with a bow and the other hit him with the butt of his gun. My father was the one who hit him with the bow. Those were war honors and you could name some child after them.[2]

Many years later one woman was looking for names for her twin girls. Those girls are Anna and Sally Moon. She went to my father. She said that she didn't want religious names. My father told her about that raid and said that names could be taken from it for the twins. They were named "Lying-Ready-to-Strike" and "Struck-Him-First." My father gave the names to them.

When they named children like that, there had to be a witness who could verify the events from which the names were taken. They were afraid to give names like that if they were not sure the events were true, because then the child would be sickly.

LONG AGO, the Apaches went to Mexico to raid for horses. They saw two men and took after them, but didn't catch them. The chief got the men together, and they decided they had better go home because their horses were tired and because the men they had chased might return with others. So they started eastward again. Those two men they chased got more men and began to trail them. The Apaches camped overnight. Before noon of the next day the white men caught up to them. There was a fight. One of the Apaches was shot in the stomach. The Apache leader said, "There are too many of them against us. We had better try to outrun them. Shoot at their horses; if we can put them on foot they will never catch us." They began shooting the white men's horses. They shot the last white man left on horseback. The white men scattered. The Apaches moved on.

During the fight, the cousin of the Apache who was shot in the stomach ran into the hills and watched the battle. After the whites

---

[2] Counting coup (French *coup*, a blow) was a common practice in Plains Indian warfare. In this instance the Kiowa Apache, who learned the custom only after reaching the Plains in the early eighteenth century, applied it against whites.

had scattered and the Indians had moved on, he came out and saw the wounded man. He saw that the wound had gone clear through him. He picked him up and said, "I'll take you into the hills." He carried the man. The man's gut could be seen; it was almost sticking out. When they got into the hills, he tied a piece of buckskin around him to hold his gut in. Then they started out on foot. He led the wounded man, supporting him and helping him to walk along. After two days they reached some water. He fixed the wounded man a bed of grass beside the water. He took a paunch water bag and filled it and washed the wounded man's face. He wouldn't give him a drink of water for fear it might run out through his wound. Then his cousin left him there and went to hunt for game. He got a deer and brought it back. He fed the wounded man, but it hurt him to eat. The cousin thought to himself that he couldn't live, and it was impossible to take him back, so he would leave in the morning and abandon him.

The next day the cousin left some meat and water for the wounded man. He didn't say he was going to leave him. He just left. He traveled on and at last he came to his camp. He saw his own mother. She thought that he had been killed, and had already started cutting herself.[3] He explained to her that the other fellow had been killed, but not he.

The wounded man lay back there, getting worse. He couldn't eat or drink, and his wounds were getting rotten. Some Comanches stopped there one night for water and to camp. They sent two men for water. Those men smelled something rotten and heard someone groan. They got their water and went back to camp. They told their chief what they smelled and heard. They said, "We don't know what it is; maybe ghosts or spirits." The two Comanches made torches out of bundles of grass, and several others went with them to look around. Finally they saw the wounded man, and one of them went back and told the chief. The chief told him to take a blanket and carry the man back in it. Then they built a big fire and laid the man down. The buckskin around his waist was getting rotten. They took some water in a turtle shell and let it drip into his mouth. They left him as he was for the night.

In the morning they gave the man water again. One man said to give him pounded meat to see if he could eat it. He ate it all right.

---

[3] That is, self-mutilation, a common mourning practice in aboriginal times.

They decided to leave two or three men to stay with him while the rest went into the mountains to look around for prickly pear. They brought some in. The chief burned off the stickers, cut the prickly pear in half, put some buffalo grease on it, and placed it over the wound. Then he tied buckskin over it. They fed the man and watched him for two days. Soon he seemed to come out of it. The chief changed the bandage and put on some more prickly pear. Then they asked him his tribe, but he couldn't understand Comanche. The chief told the rest of his people, "I can tell by the way he is dressed that he is either Kiowa or Apache." He asked the man in sign language, "What tribe are you?" The man replied, "Apache"— he made the sign for "knife sharpener." The Comanche chief said, "We have gone this far, but I hate to go on and leave this man. We will turn back and go home again." He told his men to cut two poles for a travois to take the man back on, and to get more prickly pears.

The wounded man began to eat and drink better. Early the next morning they put him on the travois and started back. They camped at night. Every once in a while they changed his bandage.

Finally they reached the Comanche camp. The Comanche chief said, "I found this boy, and from now on I will call him 'son' and his father 'brother.'" They took good care of the wounded Apache, and when he began getting stronger, he took care of the chief's horses and hunted for him. He stayed with the Comanche for a while. When the Comanche were getting ready to go west again, the Apache boy said he would go along. When they got to Mexico, he went ahead and drove some horses out of a corral. The Comanche got the horses and drove them back to their camp. The boy gave all the horses he captured to the Comanche chief.

That boy was with the Comanches nearly three years. Then they heard the Kiowa were going to have a Sun Dance and that the Apaches would be there. The chief of the Comanches called the Apache boy in. By now the boy could understand Comanche pretty well. The chief said, "You have been away from your people a long time. Now they are going to have the Sun Dance. Maybe you want to return." The Apache boy said he would go home to his people. The chief told him he could have all the horses he wanted to take back, including his own two fast ones. The boy said he would ride a red mule and lead the two horses, but that was all he would take.

The Comanche chief's wife fixed the Apache's clothes and gave him plenty of dried meat. Then he started off. He rode all day and camped on the prairie at night. He rode two days and nights all together. At noon he reached a big camp next to a creek. He rode around and tied his horses up. He rode the mule over to the spring where they got water. A woman came by for water, but she wouldn't look at him. When she got close he asked her for water. She gave him some in a turtle shell, but looked the other way. He said, "Are you scared? Don't you know me?" She said, "Yes, I know you." He asked, "Who am I?" She called his name and he said, "Yes, that's me." She asked, "Are you alive?" He said, "Sure, I'm talking to you." She said, "We heard you got killed long ago. Your mother is just beginning to look like herself again. Are you alive?" He asked where his mother's camp was. The woman told him. He asked her to tell them he was waiting for them. The woman went to her camp, put her water down, and went right on. She told her mother she was in a hurry. When she got to the man's mother's camp, she said, "I came to see you. See that man over there on horseback? That is your boy and he wants you." The old lady dropped everything and just sat there. Pretty soon she asked, "Is that true? Is he alive?" Then she went over to her husband and said, "Old man, that man there is our son." The old man asked her and the woman who brought the news if it was true. Then he ran down there. When he got close he recognized his boy. He stopped and called, "Is that you?" The boy said, "Yes, it's me."

Throughout the camps everyone heard the news. When the man's cousin heard it, he left. The man told all the people the whole story of what happened to him. After that the people went to the Sun Dance which they had been preparing for.

ONE TIME Daha's son-in-law said he was going to steal a horse near Anadarko, go south somewhere and sell it. He stayed all night near Boone at Daha's house. The next day he went to Anadarko. He was there a few days, when he got sick with a high fever and died there.

His wife got tired of waiting for her husband to return. She went to Daha and gave him a cigarette[4] and asked him to find out where her husband was. Daha asked for two men to come and sing for him. She went for them and explained to them that Daha was going to work with Owl[5] and find out where her husband had gone.

That night the two singers came. One of them was Apache Sam and the other was my wife's grandfather. They all went inside. Daha smoked his rattle in the fire, and gave a rattle to each of the singers. They let the fire die down and then they began to sing. Daha told them to sing four songs, and to finish them even if his power came before they were finished. During the third song there was a shaking noise. When they finished the last song, all became quiet again. Then they heard a tapping noise on the tipi poles. Daha just said "yes" to it. Then they heard the shaking sound again and his power left.

Daha told them to rekindle the fire. He asked Apache Sam to load the pipe again, and after they smoked he told them what he learned. He said to the woman, "You asked me to do this for you to find out where your husband went. That noise you heard was him. He said, 'I got to Anadarko and became sick and died. I am no longer on earth. I am with the old people now. Tomorrow a man and a woman will come to you on horseback, about noon.'" She began to cry. Daha told her not to cry, that they would learn more when those two people came the next day.

In the morning they watched, and about noon, two people came into camp on horseback. They sat down under a shady tree. An old man asked where they came from. They said they were from Anadarko. They said, "Daha's son-in-law got sick and died there."

The Owl was bad, but sometimes it was good, almost like a telephone, they say.

A LONG TIME AGO, when my father was just a young boy, he hadn't yet been out with the other fellows who fought and raided. There was one old man who wanted to take my father along one time. He went to my father's father and said, "Maybe your son wants to go with us this time." My grandfather said, "If he wants to go along, it is all right. But he is pretty small." My father wanted to go along,

[5] The owl was associated with supernatural power and could be called upon by a shaman for assistance.

so they told him to fix up his moccasins and bring along an extra pair, and to get his arrows ready.

They got everything ready for my father, and that night they left. Some Kiowas were along on the raid too. They traveled for several days to Mexico. There they found a place to raid for horses. They also captured a Mexican boy. They stayed down in Mexico three years. In the spring, they came back this way, driving horses and cattle. Everything was all right with them.

In the meantime, sometime during the three years the raiding party was away, some Comanches went to the Apache camp and said the party had been wiped out. When these Comanches were telling the story, Daha heard it and told his wife he had bad news. She was related to my grandfather. Daha said not to tell my grandfather that his son had been killed. He said he was going to talk to a Kiowa who knew something about Owl.

Daha went to see the Kiowa man. The Kiowa man said, "You have come for something." Daha said, "I came because I have heard bad news. You know the Owl. I want you to help us find out something. We heard that my brother-in-law's boy was killed along with some Apaches and Kiowas who went out to raid. We want you to find out."

The Kiowa man told Daha to bring him all of the tail feathers from one eagle. Daha told his wife he didn't have any eagle feathers, and asked her to go to her brother and ask for them. He said she should explain to him that they were asking the Kiowa man to find out the truth for them. Daha's wife asked her brother for the eagle feathers and explained it to him. Then he sent a man to tell all the people to stay inside their tipis while he sent Owl out to look for my father. The man called out to the people and they listened to him. He said, "Owl is going to look for a man."

The Kiowa man began to sing four songs after sundown. Everyone listened. Owl called back from west of the camp. He spoke to Owl and told him what he wanted. He said, "Go look for the lost boy." Owl listened and called back, "I understand and I will go for you."

The next morning the Kiowa man went back to Daha's camp and said the messsage had been sent.

The raiding group that my father was with was still on its way back. It was noon and they were eating, not far away. My father sat under a tree. He was feeling lonesome. A Kiowa man got up and said, "Listen, everyone. A message has been sent to us. It is flying around in the air." Then Owl alighted on top of the tree that my father was sitting under and looked down at him. The Kiowa man said, "Do not be afraid. Owl has brought us a message." He spoke to the Owl, saying, "We do not want to hear anything bad. We are all right. Go back and tell them that." The Owl circled around and flew back. It went back to the Kiowa medicine man and told him to make the people be quiet that night while he gave his message. So he sent a man out to tell all the people to be quiet.

After dark, when all was quiet, Owl called from the west side of camp. Then he flew away.

The Kiowa medicine man told all the people the message. He said, "Owl sat right above him. They are all well and will come into camp tomorrow. The boy was lonesome, but nothing else was wrong with him."

The raiding party traveled on toward home. At daylight they saw the camp. They said they would surprise the people and enter by night.

My father said he went into camp that night and found his tipi and stirred up the fire. His father slept lightly and the noise woke him up. When he recognized my father, he woke his wife and told her that their son had come home. They got up and fed him. Then his mother went outside and sang. The words of her song were about her boy coming home that night. Everybody in camp got up for their boys, and all night long they were glad for the return of their sons.

That is how Daha got Owl power. He learned it from that Kiowa man.

LONG AGO, the Apaches were camping near the North Canadian River. Some Kiowas were camping with them. To the west was a camp of Comanches, with a few Kiowas and Apaches.

One night a Kiowa man stole an Apache woman and went somewhere west with her. They went on horseback. They stayed away from camp all night and went back toward camp early the next morning. On their way this couple saw some soldiers accompanied by a few Indians, and they began to shoot at the couple. The couple got away all right. As they rode into camp, the man hollered out, "All of you, get up! We are going to be attacked." There were mostly women and children in the camp, because most of the Apache men were away somewhere on the warpath. The soldiers began attacking the camp and the people started to scatter.

The day before this attack started, the people in the Apache camp were trading with some Mexicans, and got some crackers. They wanted to get a lot of them. The Mexicans said that if they got a lot of crackers, they would get scattered all over if they should be attacked. There was a Mexican captive among the Apaches who understood what the Mexicans said. He said the Mexicans were just joking and teasing.

During the attack, the Apache children were running, some of them barefooted. It was cold. While the women were running off east to the other camp, a few Apache and Kiowa men fought the soldiers. My father said that as he started off east, his uncle came up on a horse. He was the only one with a horse, because the other people's horses were all scattered. My father and his sister took his uncle's horse. His uncle said, "Go ahead and ride, fast!" Then Big Wolf came into camp with a bunch of horses. There was one horse there that belonged to my father's uncle that was always hard to catch, but this time my father's uncle walked right up and caught him easily. The people still left in camp took these horses and went off. My father's uncle rode over to where the Kiowas and a few Apaches were fighting the soldiers. After a while, his horse was shot out from under him, and when it fell, it pinned his leg to the ground. While he was lying there, the soldiers rode up and tried to hit him with their gun butts, but he managed to duck under part of the horse. Finally, the Kiowas and Apaches drove the soldiers away from him. The word got to the people fleeing eastward that my father's uncle had been killed.

After a while my father's uncle got out from under the horse and was picked up when a Kiowa fellow rode past him. They rode back into the fight again. They rode up to one of the enemy and killed him with a spear. The enemy started to scatter. The Indians turned back. They got to a place where some horses had been left and got one for my father's uncle. Then they rode into battle again.

During the battle one woman had one of the medicine bundles.[6]

---

[6] Medicine bundles, or "worships," as the Kiowa Apache called them in English, were sacred objects among Plains Indians. Each had an outer covering of cloth or leather; inside were such objects as bits of tobacco, a pipe, pieces of cloth and leather. As with so many aspects of Kiowa Apache culture which

She got into the creek waist-deep and covered herself with moss and grass. Some of the people had fled to the hills to watch the fighting. My grandfather took his tipi, rolled it up and hid it in the brush. Big Wolf took a big sack of crackers and hid them somewhere, because the Apaches were losing the battle. There was one Apache who had a white horse; he was killed right near the camps. The enemy was nearly all around them.

The people who were fleeing eastward got to the camp over there and got the Comanches, Kiowas and Apaches there to come and help. Then they began to win the battle and the enemy started to leave.

The sister of the man who was killed right near the camps joined in the fighting. During a retreat, her horse balked. Finally the others got her horse to move by whipping it and she got away with the others.

At last the Indians got too strong for the soldiers and drove them out. Some of the Indians went back to the camps; the others decided to follow the soldiers to make sure they didn't turn back again. They followed them part of the night and then they camped.

The group of Apaches that was off on the warpath somewhere when this battle began were on their way back. They camped some distance away and sent some men on ahead to find the camp. These men saw wagon tracks and the marks of iron horseshoes. Then they saw the dead horse of the man whose horse had been shot out from under him. They saw the burned camp. They turned back. That night,

---

were acquired late in their history by cultural borrowing from Plains peoples and which did not become deeply imbedded in their traditions, memories of the medicine bundles faded rather rapidly after white contact. With the Kiowa Apache, tradition has it that there were four bundles, each entrusted to the custody of a particular family. Annually, the bundles were opened with the appropriate ceremony. At other times, an individual in distress could go to the keeper of a bundle and be permitted to address prayers to the supernatural power it was thought to contain. Circumspect behavior in the vicinity of a medicine bundle was required; one could not, for example, whistle or gamble near one. Something of this reverent attitude is conveyed by an informant's statement: "I don't talk to you about the bundles in the same way that I tell you the coyote stories. I have a different feeling inside. I believe in them [the medicine bundles]." Coyote stories tell of the foolish, reprehensible, licentious, greedy trickster figure, and were responded to by Kiowa Apache audiences with much hilarity.

when they got close to their main group, they howled like wolves and waited for a return call. That was their way of telling who they were and giving their location. They rode into camp and didn't say anything. The others there noticed that, and asked what was wrong. They said, "We don't feel well. You will see for yourself when we go tomorrow. We saw lots of horse tracks where fighting had been going on. We saw one dead horse there. We saw burned tipis and the body of one man. We turned around and came back here."

There was a woman there who had some children back where the fighting had taken place. She started to cry. Her husband said, "Do not cry. If you cry I will kill you. Every time I go somewhere, you always like to go along with me!"

They stayed up all night. At dawn they started for the place where the battle had been. When they came to the dead horse, one fellow said, "This man didn't get killed. If he had been killed there would be blood all around here. It was just his horse that was killed." Then another man spoke up: "I don't think they all got killed. You can see some of the tipis are gone, poles and all. If they had been killed here, their bodies would be here and the tipis would all be burned." They camped there that night and decided to start eastward the next day in search of the people they believed had gotten away.

They went east. After one day they reached a big camp and found their people. They told about the battle and said they lost only two men.

THIS IS A STORY that my former wife told me not very long ago. She heard it from some other people—either Comanches or Kiowas. It is about the Pawnees, long before the country opened.

A boy, his wife and his sister were camping somewhere, looking for buffalo. He put up a separate tipi for his sister, because he didn't want to be sleeping close to her. The boy found some buffalo and brought in the meat. They were slicing the meat until late that night. Then his sister went back to her tipi to go to bed. She went to sleep right away because she was tired.

That night a Pawnee sneaked into the camp. He saw the boy and his wife sleeping. He went over where the boy's sister was and had intercourse with her. The girl thought it must have been her own brother because they were out there camping by themselves, with no one else around. The Pawnee left, and the girl began to cry.

Early the next morning the boy's wife was fixing something to eat. They noticed that his sister didn't feel good. She sat there and ate, saying nothing, and went back to her tipi.

The boy told his wife, "Go over and talk to my sister. Maybe she is getting sick." The boy's wife went to her sister-in-law's tipi and asked what was wrong. The girl said, "What I have to say, I am ashamed of, and if I die, it will be all right. I want to ask you, did my brother sleep all night with you?" The boy's wife said, "Yes." Then the girl said, "This morning when I woke up, someone was lying on top of me. I think it was my brother." The boy's wife said, "I am going to ask him. If he did that, I will quit him."

She told her husband, "I know that you went to bed with me last night. Sometime during the night, did you go to your sister and have intercourse with her? If you did, I will not live with you any more. Your sister doesn't care if she dies."

The boy said, "I didn't do that. It wasn't me. You go to her and tell her to tie a rope to her wrist when she goes to bed tonight. I will tie the other end to my wrist. Tonight, when whoever it was comes there, she can pull on the rope, and when I awaken, I will pull back on it. Then she can grab him and I will come over there."

After they ate that night, the boy's wife went to his sister and said, "Do not think anything about your brother. Tonight he will catch whoever it was." The boy said, "Tell her to stay awake. I will stay awake, too. We will catch whoever it was. It must be a Pawnee; they are sure bad."

That night the boy's sister went to bed early. She took the blanket away from her body and pulled her clothes up. She lay there ready for the Pawnee. The boy slept with a gun and a sharp knife close to him. He told his wife that when his sister pulled the rope, she should follow him. He said he would go in and chase the man out and she should shoot the man then.

In the middle of the night the boy's sister heard someone coming. She lifted her dress up higher and stretched out her arms so she would be ready to grab him. The Pawnee came in and got on top of her. She pulled the rope a little. When her brother pulled it back, she grabbed the Pawnee with her arms. That was the signal that her brother was coming. She locked her legs around him. Her brother came and called, "Where is he?" He felt around and then he stabbed the Pawnee with his knife and killed him right there.

Then the boy told them to get the horses ready so they could move, because some other Pawnees might be nearby. They traveled all day. The boy said he was going back and see the Pawnee he killed. The next day he went back to the dead man, built a fire there and burned him.

III

Going to School

In 1891 I first went to school. I was already a pretty big boy. In those days a lot of the children never went to school at all. Henry Brownbear, who was a chief, went to the agent and told him he wanted all the children of school age in the tribe to go to school, and that if they didn't their parents should not get rations. Children had gone to school before this, but this was my first time. After this, the Apache parents began to put their children in school.

Before I went, my mother's brother tried to teach me the ABC's. Out of that, all I learned was the letter "s." I didn't even understand a word of English. My uncle had been to school and he used to come to our camp to teach me. He knew I was going to have to go to school some day.

When September came I knew it was time for school, but I didn't know what day of the month it began. My father took me on horseback to the Kiowa School. He took me first to the camp at Anadarko when they went to get the rations. They used to go to Anadarko every two weeks for rations and camp there. When my father took me to school from the camp I had long hair and was dressed in buckskin. I was really dressed up. My father took me in to the superintendent and introduced me into the school. The superintendent sent me over to the playroom for the big boys. There was another Apache boy there who spoke good English. His name was Logan.

The first thing they did was to cut my hair. There were a lot of boys in there having that done. They took off my buckskin and gave me a shirt. My hair was long and braided, just like it is now. They took a scissors and cut the braids off and gave them to my father. Then they trimmed my hair short all around. This boy Logan acted as an interpreter for the Apache boys there. He took me into a place where they gave me a bath.

After I was all cleaned up and ready, I went back to the superintendent and waited for him. I was all dressed up in school clothes.

83

I had black pants and my shirt was blue with stripes. The superintendent came in. He said my name was going to be James. My father took all my other clothes that I had come there with and rolled them up in a bundle. He said he was going home.

I had to wait in the big boy's playroom. When it was getting toward noon I saw all the other boys coming down from upstairs where the schoolroom was. Logan was still with me. He told me that when the first bell rang, we would go to eat. He said that when we got down there he would tell me what do do. The second bell had rung and we were going to dinner. We all lined up according to height. Logan told me to watch the others, who had been there some time already. Some fellow there gave a command that I didn't understand, and I saw all the others were standing there at attention with their arms at their sides. Then this fellow said something else and we all turned. This fellow would hit a bell he was carrying and we were supposed to march in time to it. I didn't know at the time what it was for. My legs just wouldn't do it so I started walking. When we got to the eating place, there were long tables there in rows. Logan was still with me. When we got to a certain table he told me to just stand there. There was a lady there in charge who had a little bell and, when she hit it, everybody sat down. I was going according to what Logan told me. I watched the others and did what they did. After we sat down they rang the bell again and everybody had his head bowed. I guess they were asking the blessing. Everybody had his head down but I didn't hear anyone giving the prayer. The bell rang again and we started eating. I noticed that the sweet potatoes were cooked differently from what I was used to. I had always eaten them baked whole in the fire, but these were boiled. It was a good dinner. We had bacon and beans, plums and dried peaches.

Logan went to school only a half day, and he worked for the school in the afternoon. He was an interpreter, and he also worked in the barn.

When the meal was over the bell was rung. We stood up again, and when they rang the bells once more, we marched out in time to a bell. We went back to the playroom where our hats were hung. We took our hats and all went out to play. That afternoon while we were playing, Logan spoke to the schoolteacher. Then Logan told me that when the bell rang again, to go back into the playroom. They were playing around with a ball and chasing each other. I felt like a stranger and just stood around and watched the others. They played at throwing arrows. There were some stakes in the ground and they threw arrows to see who could come the closest. It was something like horseshoes. Some of the boys played marbles. We went back into the building when the bell rang. All the boys hid their playthings. Logan was told that he didn't have to work that afternoon but was to interpret and show the new fellows what to do.

They rang the bells again and we marched upstairs to the chapel. There were desks in rows there and we all sat down. They played some music and everybody sang. When they were through singing a lady came in and picked out her class and they went off to another room. One lady after another came in to get her class and they went off. All that were left were us beginners. Finally our teacher came in and took us to a room. We sat down at desks. Logan sat right beside me. They all had slates in their desks. The lady said something and they all pulled the slates out of their desks. There was none in my desk. There were erasers in their desks, but I didn't have one. All the pupils took yellow-looking books out of their desks. The teacher took a board and hung it up in front of the class. On it were pictures of birds and cats. They had letters under them, I guess, but I didn't know what they were. The teacher brought over a box that was full of wooden sticks, something like matches, all different colors. She explained them to Logan, and he told me I was to go ahead and play with them and build things, like houses and a fence. Over on the other side of the room was the part of the class that was learning to read. The teacher would point to the pictures on the wall and call the name of the animal, and the class would repeat it after her. But over on my side, where there were just beginners, I was playing with those wooden blocks. After a while it was recess and everybody put away his books. I put my box of blocks in the desk. Before we went back after recess Logan said to me, "Now you know what you are supposed to do. You're on your own now." When we got back to the classroom the teacher said something which I couldn't understand. I took out those blocks and started playing with them again like before.

Things went on like that day after day.

I don't know how long it was after I started school when Logan came over and said they were going to take my blocks and give me a slate. They gave me a slate and something that looked like a bone. That was a slate pencil. Logan told me that whenever the teacher pointed to something on the wall and said a word afterward, I should say it. Some of the boys already knew these birds and animals and could point them out by themselves. They had passed this and were already on another page, but I was behind, only beginning to learn.

When the teacher pointed to me one time and said, "Come on," I knew what that meant because the other boys had taught me that on the outside. I went up there and it was my turn to repeat after her when she pointed to a picture and called the name out. I knew what I was supposed to do because Logan had told me on the outside. After a while I could take the pointing stick and go up and point to the different pictures and call the names. I would point to them and say, "My cat," "My dog," "My bird." I was learning fast now. When we went out to play I would see real birds and call out "Bird." When they turned the chart over, it had letters down one side, and on the other side there were words like "cat" and "dog." I learned how to spell these words. When I had learned my ABC's and knew how to print them, I could spell these words out in writing. When we got to the third page, it was harder. There were whole lines of letters and words. I remember it said, "Mr. Rat has a black feather on his head." This was pretty hard for me.

The next year when I went back to school, I was given a little yellow book. I had learned all of that chart already.

All of my first year in school I felt like a stranger. I never mixed with the other kids much and so I stayed out of all the mischief. I always minded the teacher and did just what I was taught. After a while I began to get better acquainted. This was my second year. I was issued a book and paper and pencil. One of the girls in my class began to tease me. One day I was writing my lesson, and she was sitting right across the aisle. She would get up and look over at what I was writing and say, "Oh, you are wrong." I saw her chewing some paper. Pretty soon something hit me back of the ear, and I saw a piece of paper on the floor. I picked it up and put it in my desk. She began writing again, and I was watching her. I reached in my desk and took that paper wad and threw it and hit her right on the cheek. All that time the teacher must have been watching me. She caught me and called out my name and that girl's name, and she told us to behave. I went about my work again, but as soon as she turned her back, that girl threw another paper wad and hit me on the face. I kind of got mad and I didn't care—I just picked it up and stood up and hit her right in the face with it. The teacher came over and got that girl and put her in the corner and told her not to turn around. She did the same thing to me, too. We stood in the corner about an hour, right through the recess, until about noon. After everyone had gone for dinner, she told us two to go ahead and eat. That was the first time I ever got punished.

I ran away from school three times. The first time I did it, it was in the morning before breakfast. Two other Apache boys came to me and said, "Let's go home to camp. They are going to butcher today. Today they get the rations."[1] They used to have a roll call after breakfast, up in the chapel. When they called the roll that morning, they found out that three of us were missing. I knew that this was ration day and that they were going to let us go home right after the roll call. Friday was ration day, and they always let us go. I don't know why I wanted to go back early like that. I guess I wanted to be back in time for the butchering. When school was let out and the other boys came to camp, they told us three who had run off that we were supposed to go back to school that night. Everybody was supposed to be back on the evening of a ration day. I went back that night, but the other two boys didn't. They were Bill Day and Abraham Lincoln. Bill Day was Old Man Whitebone's cousin. Abraham Lincoln doesn't have any descendants living today. When we all got back to school, we went to chapel for another roll call to see who didn't come back. There were several boys and girls missing, including the other two that had run off with me. But when they called me, I answered. They gave me a choice of punishments. They said that I could spend all the next day, Saturday, sitting alone in the chapel and that I could only go down to eat. Or else I could take a whipping on the palm of my hand. I thought that a whipping would hurt, so I decided to sit up in the chapel all day long. So on Saturday, right after breakfast, they took me up to the chapel and told me that if I had to go to the toilet I should ask a certain fellow in another room to take me. I just sat there all day long. They didn't give me anything to read or play with. I would get up every once in a while and walk around the room,

[1] These were periodic distributions of foodstuffs by the federal government.

but I didn't want to go out either door. I just stayed in that chapel. Right after dinner all the other kids came to the playroom to get their caps and went home. All except me. I had to stay up there. I felt pretty bad and cried some. Pretty soon someone came in the door; it was Logan. He said, "See, you're being punished. All the other kids have gone home. I'm going down after beef. I will see if I can get permission to take you along." Logan went to the superintendent and asked if he could take me along. He told the superintendent that he needed someone to hold his team while he loaded the beef into the wagon. The superintendent said that it was all right but to make me work all day and even to help get water. I was sure glad that they let me go. We went to the barn and got the horses ready. It was a long way to go, over east of the old agency, where we were going to get the meat. When we got down there, I just sat and held the team while Logan and another fellow did all the loading. We took our time getting back. We stopped in a store in Anadarko and bought some candy. We got back to school, and another fellow there helped Logan unload the meat. Then we went back for another load. After we brought the second load back, we took three barrels and went after water, north of Anadarko, to the Washita River. We drove the wagon right into the water and dipped a bucket down into the river to fill the barrels. When we got back to school again, we poured the water into the trough for the hogs. We were just taking our time at it, and it was getting toward evening and almost time to quit. Logan said we would go down for a final load of water and when we got back we would park our wagon and unhitch the horses, and then we would quit for the day. We put up the horses in the barn, and I went back to school. Logan took me to the superintendent, who asked him how I worked. Logan said that I did all right. The superintendent said, "All right, you've had your punishment. You don't have to go back upstairs any more. You can play down here." Logan took me to the store; the superintendent had said that Logan was to get me back by sundown. This was the first big trouble I had in school. The other two fellows that had run off with me didn't come back for three days. They got the same punishment the next weekend, but they got punished for three days—Friday, Saturday, and Sunday, they didn't get to go anywhere.

It was about three months after that that I ran off again. This time there were two other boys who coaxed me into doing it. They said there was going to be a big hand game at camp. My folks were down at Boone, so I stayed in camp with the other boys' folks. Logan and a white boy working at the school came to camp in a wagon, looking for us fellows who had run away. They were afraid that we might freeze somewhere or maybe die. They were responsible for us and had to find us. They found us in camp. I didn't want to go back, but I had to. They took us up before the superintendent. It was a weekday. The superintendent gave me a choice of taking a whipping or working for two days with the girls in the school laundry. I thought I'd better work in the laundry. I had to work there two days. It was hard work. I had to work at washing dirty socks. There was a Kiowa woman boss there. I wanted to have a good time with those girls in the laundry, but that Kiowa woman boss kept watching me. The other two boys had to carry wood in to all the rooms. That was their punishment. I think I didn't get punished badly because Logan was my father's cousin's son, and he would speak to the superintendent for me. I tried to behave myself, but these other boys were always getting me into trouble. Every day I had to put on an apron and wash clothes. The girls there made fun of me. I couldn't help it. Some of those dirty socks and girl's underdrawers sure did stink. I had to help the girls carry out the tubs of dirty water and dump them. That was hard work. Those girls would tease me and say, "We've got a boy here who sure can wash good!" They let me go about noon to eat dinner. In the afternoon, I worked from one o'clock until about three-thirty. Then we had to dump out the dirty water, and at four o'clock they let me go again. The next day I had to go through the same thing all over again. By four o'clock, my punishment was over, and they let me go.

One time a bunch of us went down to the hog lot and began hitting the hogs and chasing them around. A fellow there caught us and took us to school. They took us out to the sweet-potato patch, and we all had to fill sacks with sweet potatoes and load them onto a wagon. The oldest one in the bunch of us, his name was Jerry, said that if we went back to school afterward we would surely all get whipped. He said that we should go back to the barn with a wagon and then run off. That's what we did. It wasn't ration day, so I just stayed with some boys in the camp. The next day we left camp and went north by the river. We didn't want to hang around camp because there were policemen around there. We didn't return until late at night. The superintendent had reported to the police that seven boys had run off from school. Early the next morning, two policemen came to the camp and found all of us. They took us to the agent's office, and there the policemen sent word to the school. They came down in a buggy from the school to get us. From the school they took us out to Mr. Bight, who was in charge of all the boys who were out working. They were hauling dirt down to the barn. All day I had to do this work. I had to do this hard work for three days. After supper on the third day, the superintendent came in and gave Mr. Bight a strap. He told him to give us each ten licks. The superintendent's name was Mr. Larson. Mr. Bight told him that we boys had worked hard three days and that we were tired. He said he wasn't going to beat us on top of it. The superintendent said, "You are going to whip them. You're going to do as I tell you." The superintendent was kind of a small fellow, and Mr. Bight was pretty big. The superintendent was going to fight him for not obeying his orders. Mr. Bight said, "You're just a little fellow." The superintendent struck Mr. Bight. Mr. Bight knocked him down and started beating him up. He grabbed his leg and started dragging him. Mr. Larson began crying. A fellow by the name of Clark came by and said, "That's enough." Mr. Larson got up and ran back to his office. Mr. Bight told us we weren't going to get any whipping and to go ahead and play.

Later on they were having some kind of a hearing about this fight. The agent said that he had heard that Mr. Larson had treated the boys pretty badly at the school, and so they fired Mr. Larson as school superintendent. Mr. Clark took over Mr. Larson's job until they sent out another man to take charge of the school.

My father heard about the trouble I had been in, and he told me, "Now you see what you have done. Stay out of trouble, and don't run off." After that, I never ran away from school again.

I don't remember if it was the second or third year in school, when one day I got a note. I couldn't read it. I had someone read it for me, and it was from a girl who said she wanted me to be her sweetheart. I told the fellow to write a note back to her for me and say it was all right with me. After that, whenever I would meet this girl, I would talk with her. She was a Comanche girl.

One night in the school dining hall, they had an affair in which each of the boys was sitting with a girl. They played music, and we walked around in pairs. The girls had done the inviting of the boys to this affair. They were going to pick out the best couple there. Before this affair took place, we boys were in the playroom, and a fellow came there and read out the names of certain boys that had been invited by the girls. My name was on the list. He told us to put on our Sunday clothes for this event. That evening we all got haircuts and took baths and got dressed up and ready to go. They gave us shoe polish to shine our shoes with.

On the night of this event, we were all in the playroom. When they rang the bell, all the boys who had not been invited went into the dining hall and were seated around the room. When the second bell rang, we all got ready to go in. We had hair oil on our hair, and we had flowers in our buttonholes, handkerchiefs in our pockets, and our neckties all tied. All of us boys marched in by twos. We stood real straight and had our coats buttoned up. There were about ten of us, and we were all seated on a bench in a row. We were facing a big crowd of all the students there. I noticed that there was a chalk line drawn around the floor along the edges where we were all seated. Pretty soon, as we were sitting, all the girls came in dressed in white, with red flowers on. They were sure pretty. My heart was just shaking. I didn't know which was the girl who had invited me. The girls knew who they had invited, and they each sat down beside the boy they invited. A girl came over and sat down by me. I just sat there real straight. It was the Comanche girl who had written me that note before. Someone got up and talked, and then the couples started walking around the chalk line. There were two prizes: the first one was a big cake, and a scarf and gloves; the second prize was a cake and a scarf. There was music as we went around, and we had to keep in time with the music. After we had made a complete circle, we sat down again. There were some judges there. They picked two couples and asked them to march around once again to see which was the better couple. My girl friend and I were one of the couples. I knew the other couple could march better, but the girl in that couple was chewing gum. When the judges made their decision, they said that the boy in the other couple was taller than his girl but they marched well. But they didn't like her to be chewing gum, so they gave my girl and me the first prize. They cut the cake in half and divided it between us. I got the gloves and the scarf. Then they told all the others there to go ahead and talk with their girl friends.

I was about fifteen years old at this time. It was the first time I ever had a date with a girl and talked with her like that.

My eyes bothered me. Those days all the children seemed to have sore eyes. I lost the sight in my left eye. I was taken to the eye doctor, and he said that I had bad eyes. They told the agent about it. After that they never bothered me about going back to school. For about two years my eyesight was very dim. I stayed close to home then. I didn't do much of anything. They took me to an Indian woman doctor. She took a piece of glass from a bottle and cut away some white substance that was growing over my left eye. After that I could see better. After she had cured me, my father gave this woman a horse. That was more valuable than money then. Some of the Apache doctors then would require you to bring four things,[2] but this woman didn't. She gave me some stuff, like salt, from the creek and something else to mix with it and told me to put this in my eye. I used this until I saw that my eyesight was all right, and then I quit. I would just go around to dances and visiting, but I never returned to school.

I think that it was in 1892 during my second school year that I experienced my first Christmas. I had never heard of Christmas before. My first year in school, they didn't have any. I began to hear people around school talking about having Christmas. I didn't know what it meant. One day some of the older boys were butchering hogs. They said that they were going to have them for Christmas dinner. I saw them bringing in a cedar tree. "Tomorrow we will have Christmas dinner," they said.

The next day we were getting ready for the dinner. The parents of the children all came to the school that morning. Upstairs the older boys were decorating the tree. About eleven o'clock they called all the children together to get cleaned up. The first bell rang. I was in the smallest group of boys. We all went out in groups to the dining room. I saw the tables all lined up with food. There were turkeys, chickens, beef, pork, and oranges and apples. It was at this dinner that I first heard a prayer at the mealtime. The same old man that later married me was the one who prayed. I didn't understand what he was praying about—he was just talking. When he finished, we began to eat. We went back to the building after eating and played outside. There was no school that day. That evening the bell rang

2 It was traditional to offer a shaman four valuable things when seeking his aid in curing illness.

earlier than usual. We went to our rooms. When the second bell rang, the different groups went upstairs. Our group was the first. We went into the chapel. We were all seated. There was a wire stretched from wall to wall with a sheet over it. We sang and prayed. A man came in about that time. He had a lot of whiskers. One of the lady teachers went up by Santa Claus and called out the names of the interpreters. Logan went up there. He said that those of us having our first Christmas would be called out and that Santa Claus would give us some things from his sack. There were ten boys seated beside the tree who were going to call out the names and give out the presents. Logan said, "Those who are having their first Christmas will get a present." The Kiowa and Comanche interpreters said the same thing. Santa Claus began to reach into his sack and pull out the presents, and as the names were called, the different interpreters would take them and give them to the right boy. My name was called. My present had candy, cakes, nuts, and a scarf, gloves, and shirt in it. I just said, "I guess this is Christmas." After the presents were given out, they took down the sheet and I saw the Christmas tree. My eyes went wide open. I really was looking at it. I think this was one of the biggest Christmases I ever saw. The girls were given shawls, and all the boys got scarves, shirts and trousers. These were the presents that were on the tree.

After the presents were handed out, we were told that the next day we could go home for about fifteen days and then we were to come back to school. That was the first Christmas I ever saw.

WHEN I FIRST got started in school they showed me where I was to sleep. It was in one big room where all the boys slept that were the same size as I was. I had to sleep with another boy, named Earl. The beds were made every day by women who worked there—we didn't have to do that. Logan showed me where I was to stay. He said I would find bedclothes under the pillow of my bed. He told me that in the morning I should always wait for the bell to ring before starting to get dressed. He explained to me that when everybody was in bed at night a man would come and see that we all had our nightshirts on. Then he would say "Good night" and turn out the lights. No one could talk after that. Logan told me that the first bell in the morning was for the boys who were to build fires in different parts of the school. The second bell was the signal for us to get dressed.

During the night we didn't go out to the toilet. They had buckets on the inside for us to use. When we got up in the morning we were supposed to fold our nightshirts and put them under the pillow. Otherwise the women who made the beds would report us. Then we were supposed to go to the playroom and wait. Each tribe had an interpreter for those of us who didn't know any English. When we got to the playroom another fellow took charge of us. I knew what to do, except where to go to wash. When Logan came in, he told me. There was a big room with pans to wash in, and pitchers full of water. We had to wash our faces, necks, and ears. I had a comb and was supposed to part my hair on the left side. When they had first cut my hair they parted it in the middle, so that confused me at first. When we were through washing we sat in the playroom in seats that were assigned to us. We waited for the next bell. I was told to do exactly what the others did when the white man gave orders.

Nobody ever talked after lights were out at night. It was shortly after dark when we went to bed. There was a kind of night watchman who walked around outside listening.

In school they watched you pretty closely to see how you behaved and how you caught on to things. When they thought you knew how, they would give you different jobs to do. I was in the playroom one day when they gave me my first job. They told me, "Tomorrow, at the first bell in the morning, you are to get up and help build the fires. In the evening you are to help cut kindling." I was also told that after breakfast I was to help the boy I slept with in sweeping up the classroom. We were supposed to clean out the desks and dust off the books.

I didn't like the jobs they gave me, but I knew that if I did them all right they wouldn't bother me. But if I didn't, they might whip me.

I kept that first job three weeks. They would change you over to a new job every few weeks. My next was to help wait on the table I sat at during meals. At each table there were two boys, one at each end, who had to go to the kitchen and bring the food. Then when everybody had eaten, those who did that work for the different tables got together to eat.

My next job was in the kitchen where they threw away the garbage.

All of these jobs were in addition to going to school all day. Later on I worked half a day and went to school half a day.

Once I had a job going through the buildings picking up the dirty sheets and nightshirts the women left in baskets after they made the beds. That job ended about springtime. Then I was sent in a group of six boys to wash dishes over in the building where the teachers and employees ate. We got to eat there, too. The food was much better there. They had chicken and pie sometimes. That was my last job before school let out.

Just about a week before school let out for the summer, all the kids were put to work to clean the whole school out. There were no classes that week. We wore our work clothes and worked all the time. While we were getting things cleaned up for the closing of school, we had to clean up our clothes and get them folded up. Then they were put in a basket and taken away. We had three kinds of clothes—work clothes, school clothes and Sunday clothes. Sunday clothes were made of gray material, and included a straw hat. Every morning before school we had to shine our shoes. If they weren't shined up good you had to keep shining until they were good.

The day school let out our parents were notified and they came to get us. Before noon sometime we all got together in the chapel to sing. Then we were turned loose for the summer.

When I was home that summer I felt kind of funny toward those kids who hadn't gone to school. They still had long braids. I combed my hair and kind of showed off to them. I used to tell the boys the names of things in English that I learned in school. I would sing the tunes of songs I learned, but I didn't know the words. One was that song "Jesus Loves Me." The old people thought I was smart but I didn't really know what I was singing about. I played during that summer; we shot birds and went hunting with dogs. We gathered a lot of wild plums, too.

In the second year of school I had jobs that took half days to do. I went back to school early that year. My job was to clean out the barns in the afternoons. I hauled manure and watered and fed the hogs. I did all kinds of farm work.

Then I was sent to work at the laundry helping wash clothes. Later I was a carpenter's helper, sawing up boards and sorting them out according to size. Sometimes I fixed fences. I went to school only in the mornings.

The best job I had in school was that one when I worked at the employees' building washing dishes. There I got the best food to eat. I didn't like that job at the laundry at all. I had to put a cloth over my nose and mouth because of the smell of those dirty socks. But I was kept on that job the longest of any.

When I worked at carrying meat from the butchering place to the kitchen I used to steal some of it. We helped each other at stealing meat and hiding it down by the creek. On Saturdays we would get together there and build a fire to cook it. I didn't know just where they hid it. My part in it was to steal it from the butchering place and pass it on to the others who hid it. I would fill up my pockets with dried fruit, too. There was an Apache boy in charge at the butchering place, and he helped us and was just as bad as the rest of us. His name was Jerry. Sometimes we dug up sweet potatoes and stole them, too. I think the reason we stole food was that we wanted to cook it our own way, roasted in the ashes. We never took any food to our sleeping quarters, though, because those women who cleaned up would find it and we would get punished. My father's brother worked for the school and we used to give him food to take home. I never got caught at stealing food. We were pretty careful about it.

In spring I was sent to drive a team in the plowing work. I helped with the planting, too. I learned about farming in school, and to this day I have used that knowledge in planting my garden every spring. At that time we made the furrows first, and then we went across them and planted corn at the intersections of the furrows and lines marked across them. We didn't have the machines like nowadays, that plant as you make the furrows. It was tiresome work, and we took our time, never hurrying at it.

I helped to harvest wheat at school, too. The machine would only cut the wheat, and other fellows would come along and tie it. It took a long time. When we got down to the last bunch of wheat still standing, everyone forgot about the work and started chasing rabbits they knew were in there. About four o'clock we quit working and went swimming in the creek to get cleaned up.

By my third year in school, I was experienced at all the jobs and knew what to do.

About 1893 while I was in school, there was a measles epidemic. There was a boy named Bill Day who ran off from school in the spring. When they brought him back he was sick and they took him to the school clinic. Several more boys got sick. Earl, the boy I slept with, and I had to empty bedpans in the clinic.

Bill Day was put into a room by himself. His face was full of red spots. When the other boys who were sick were getting well, they began to break out with red spots. More and more boys were catching it. Every day we would be out playing, and several more boys would come down with the measles. The clinic upstairs got so full they began putting them in the dormitories, where we slept. There were only a few of us still attending school. The boys with the measles began dying, one or two a day. The doctor and nurse were working day and night. Some of the older boys helped them give medicine. Then they began sending the boys home. When I got home the measles broke on me. The measles spread around and more children got sick. My second younger brother died from the measles.

The older people didn't understand what the measles were. They said that it was when the little spots went into your body that it killed you. I was sure sick with the measles but somehow I got well. Some of our people mixed red paint and grease and rubbed it over the children to try to cure them. The old Indians said the measles was the white man's sickness and that they never had it before the white people came.

IV

Sex, Marriage and Divorce

ONE TIME, when I was a young boy, I went hunting with Big Alex's boy. He and I were just friends. There was a girl at the camp where he stayed. She was Apache Jack's wife's brother's daughter. When he and I decided to go raccoon hunting, she wanted to go along. She was older than us. I was a young fellow, just beginning to think about sex. Big Alex's boy had a Mexican jack-mule. We rode it, and she walked. We went down by the creek. Our dog began to bark, and we saw three raccoons up in a tree. Big Alex's boy had a Winchester rifle, and he shot all three of them. We loaded them on the mule and went on. We sat down to rest, and this girl began talking nasty. She asked me if I knew anything about intercourse. I told her I didn't know where I could have any. She told me to come to the arbor near camp that night.

When we got back to camp, we skinned the raccoons and hung them up to dry. Big Alex's boy and I went down by the creek and he told me, "She's sure good. She'll show you all about it."

At sundown, we ate dinner. Apache Jack and his wife went away. There were just three of us in that camp—Big Alex's boy, that girl, and I. He went into the tipi, and she and I were left in the arbor. She lay down and raised up her dress. My penis was already stiff. I got on top of her. It didn't take long and I was through. Then I went to the tipi, and Big Alex's boy went there and had intercourse with her. He came back to the tipi and we stayed there a while, telling stories. Every once in a while we would go in there and have intercourse with that girl. I don't know how many times I did it that night. Years ago, they used to tell a story that if you had intercourse when you were too young, your penis would be bitten off by the teeth in the woman's vagina. But after I did it that first time I was all right. I liked it. After that I used to go around to dances just looking for women to have intercourse with. My father used to tell me not to run around because some of the women might have a disease. But I never got a disease; I was lucky, I guess. After the country opened up, a lot of boys went to the hospital with that kind of disease, but they never would talk about it. Then I was more careful. I didn't go around just anywhere; I was careful which girls I went with.

One time I got caught right in the act of having intercourse with a woman. That time Henry Moon's wife was sick. I went to visit them. I took my buggy and went that way. Henry and his wife were staying with a certain woman. She fixed a bed on the north side of the room for me. Henry and his wife were on the other side. This woman lay down by me. During the night she wanted to have intercourse with me. I got on top of her. The bedspring made a noise. Suddenly Henry came across the room with a lantern and called, "Hey, have you got a match?" This woman I was having intercourse with just yelled out, "No! I haven't got any match!" Henry didn't want a match; he just wanted to know what was going on with that woman and me.

IT WAS in my third year at school that I met Louisa, the girl that I later married. I used to talk with her when I met her. After my eyes got bad, I was at home most of the time. I never saw much of her. When my eyes got better, I used to see her up at Anadarko and I would talk with her. I guess it was during the summertime, when school was out, that I was going around looking for girls. I saw her at a store in Anadarko. I started going with her. I went with lots of girls, but I always had this one on my mind. I went around with her, but I was afraid to marry her because she was younger than I. I was afraid of the agent because then you weren't supposed to marry anyone unless she was of age. This girl was still young. When school was ready to begin again, I heard that she was going to go back to Chiloco, and when I asked her about it, she said that she was going to sign up for three years. That hurt my feelings. All the school kids that were going to go away to school came down to the Riverside School to spend the night there. I went over there on horseback. There was a big crowd there. I saw her there, but I couldn't get to talk with her. So I just went back to my camp. She went away. I heard, during her third year away at school, that the school kids were going to arrive at Chickasha in July and that on the third and fourth of July there would be a big time there. The Indians were invited to take part in it. I went over to the depot, and all the women folks were there waiting for the train to arrive with their children. The men were dancing. She wasn't on that train, and I heard that it would be night before another train would come. I went back down to the campgrounds and took part in the dance. We were all being paid for dancing. We were doing all kinds of dancing. I danced late that night and went back to camp to sleep. The other people who were expecting children to arrive had gone back to the depot.

The next morning my mother fixed me breakfast. My mother told me that the train had come in the night before, with more kids from school. On the fifth of July, when they were breaking camp and packing up to go to Anadarko, I looked around and saw this girl. I was watching her. She and another girl got into a buggy. Louisa was driving it. I saw them leave. When they got a little distance off, I got on my horse and followed them. There were others coming behind me. Another fellow who was married rode up to me and asked if I had seen Louisa. I told him I hadn't but that I was going to let her get just so far along and when the wagons got scattered out, I would wait my chance and ride up to her wagon. I saw the chance after a while and kicked my horse. I rode right up to her. I didn't want to go up before that time because I was afraid of her folks and anybody else that might see me. I rode up and cut right up in front of the wagon and called to her to stop. I noticed that she looked at me and smiled. I said, "Remember how we used to talk before you went off to school? Is everything all right, just as it was before? If it is, we will go on from here together." She said it was still all right. She said that they were going to stop west of Verden to eat and that when she and her girl friend went down for water, I should go down there and we would talk. When I got there and everybody was ready to eat, I just got off my horse and climbed into a wagon and watched her. She and her girl friend got out of their wagon and went on down to the creek. Her father and mother unhitched her horses. I got on my horse again and rode down to the creek. When I got there, these two girls were sitting under the shade of a tree. When I got off my horse, we began to talk. I said, "When we get back to Anadarko, we will get married right away. I don't want to wait. You might start running around and getting crazy." She agreed to that. She said that when she got back she would take off her school clothes and put on her Indian dress and then we would be married. When we got through talking, we ate dinner in camp there and went on to

Anadarko. We reached Anadarko that evening. When we camped for the night, I went around and saw my other girl friends. When the camp broke up the next morning and everyone went home, Louisa went to her folks' place, just east of where Big Joe lives now. I went home to Boone. I stayed around home two or three weeks, and I didn't see her at all. Everybody was getting ready to go back to Anadarko for rations again. They camped where the airport is now. The Apaches camped on the south. The Comanches and Kiowas were camping around there, too. I saw Louisa and her girl friend going in a buggy up north of Anadarko to get rations there. That was the first time I saw her in Indian clothes since she returned from school. I followed them on horseback. She went on east, to where the store was. I followed her there. She was sitting on a bench in front of the store, and when I got there I sat down beside her. I said, "Now you must make up your mind. Go back with me, and we will get married in the real Indian way. After we stay together awhile, we will go to the Agency. I will be down by your camp tonight. I will be nearby. I will be waiting for you. From there we will go on and spend the night out in the timber. Then we will come back."

When I got back to camp, I told my father's sister that I was going to steal that girl that night. I told her that in the morning when the people found that this girl was gone, they would know it was I who stole her. I ate supper that evening, but I didn't tell my folks what I was up to. I changed into my old clothes. I was in a hurry. A little after dark I went out there. It was our plan that when I got to where we were to meet, I would light a cigarette and she would meet me. It wasn't long after I lit a cigarette that she came over to me. We went on west a ways and spent the night down in the timber.

Early in the morning I took Louisa out a little ways farther and told her to wait while I went back to camp and got some food. She told me to be sure to return and not leave her out there alone. When I got to camp, people had already eaten and were sitting around talking. They were all talking about Louisa because they knew she was gone. They were asking around at different camps about her. My mother asked me if I saw this girl anywhere, and I told her that I hadn't. I asked her to put up some crackers and some canned goods. When she asked where I was going, I just told her that I was going off somewhere for a while. I brought in my horse and got it saddled and ready. I knew that my father now knew what I was up to. My

father said, "I know what it is, son. You don't even have to tell me.
That girl who is gone—you are the one who stole her. Now, son, you
bring her back here today. Don't go off anywhere else with her." I
said, "No, I don't know anything about her." I took the food my
mother prepared and left. Later on, I heard from my father's sister
that right after I had left, an old lady came into camp asking for me.
My aunt told her that I had left just a while before. When I got back
to Louisa, we ate the food and went over by the river. We waited
there until late at night. Then we rode back to the camp. I always
had a tent there, right beside my father and mother. After the people
in camp missed Louisa, they learned that I was the only young man
gone from camp.

The next morning, that same woman who had come into camp
asking for me, Louisa's mother's sister,[1] came looking for Louisa.
She found her in my tent. She was mad. She told Louisa, "This
young man here you are going to marry, I don't like him. He has too
many women that he has thrown away. He will do the same to you."
I said nothing. I just sat there. She asked Louisa to go with her, and
when she refused, she took Louisa by the wrist and pulled
her.

My father's sister said to me, "I like that girl. Today we will go
home. You go see her and bring her over to my place."

Louisa's mother's sister took her over to her camp, and from
there they loaded up and went back to Louisa's home, east of Big
Joe's present place. Her aunt was afraid I would steal her
again.

We stayed around the ration camp awhile, and then we moved home
again. I didn't go to see her. Next ration day everybody went back to
camp again. Louisa, her mother, and two of her mother's sisters
were eating together, and with them was a brother of theirs, called
Colonel. He said to the women, "Louisa is my niece. She is not
crazy, and she doesn't run around. When she came back from school,
she got married. Now you've gone and taken her away from her
husband. Now maybe she will just stay around here and run around
and get pregnant, without a husband. I want you to take her back to
her husband." He spoke directly to Louisa's mother. "You are my
sister. I want you to take my niece back to him. I don't want you to

[1] Mother's sister was called by the same kinship term as mother. A girl's
maternal aunt would tend to be concerned with her welfare.

break my word. You are her mother. It is up to you to take her back."
They called him Big Wolf. He was Louisa's mother's sister's husband. They told him to go to my mother's camp and bring her over
to get her daughter-in-law. We were sitting eating and talking when
Big Wolf came in. They asked him if he had eaten. He said, "No,
I didn't come for that. I have something to tell you. I came to get
you to go over and bring your daughter-in-law back." My mother
said she would ask me if I still wanted her. She said that if I didn't
she wouldn't go over. My mother came in and told me that Big Wolf
had come and what he wanted her to do. I told my mother to go
over there and that if that was the way they wanted it, to bring her
back. I watched my mother as she left to go over there. My mother
went inside Louisa's tent. The others at that camp were sitting out
under the arbor. Pretty soon I saw my mother coming with Louisa. I
just went back and lay down on my bed. The door opened, and I heard
my mother say to Louisa, "Go on in." When she came in, I told her
to sit down. She was just smiling. We were both glad to be together
again. Right then we considered ourselves married, in the Apache
way.

   About a month after we were together, they were going to give out
money at the Agency to the head of each family. My mother-in-law
went in to get her money. As the agent gave her money, he was
checking off the names of her children. He said, "This daughter,
Louisa, she is now of age. Let her come for her own money. Call
her in." She told the agent that Louisa was married. The agent
asked whom she married. Louisa's mother said that she had married
me. The agent then said that the only way that Louisa could get
money was for her to come in with her husband. He said that they
would issue a ticket for Louisa and me. The agent went and got my
father and talked with him. He asked my father if his boy was
married. He told my father to tell me to come here with my wife and
that then they would send us over to Mr. Methvin's place to have
him marry us. Then we were to come back to be issued a payment
ticket. That money they were giving out was from the grassland
leases. My father explained this to me, and my wife and I went in a
buggy to see the agent. He told us that Mr. Methvin would pray for
us and give us a paper.[2] When we got the paper, we were supposed
to get our money. They gave us the money and a ration ticket.

   [2] That is, a marriage license.

IT WAS about two years or so after I was married that I had my first experience with drinking. A lot of fellows then used to go to Chickasha or to Wichita Falls to get liquor. I never drank then. When all of these towns around here first started, there were fellows there in long tents who would sell whisky. That was before they put up buildings. Over at Hatchetville we had a big Ghost Dance camp. At the camp I used to see them drinking and gambling. They would get the stuff in town, and you could see them drinking along the road on the way back. A lot of fellows who are still living, like Big Joe, Alfred Kipling, and Whitebone, drank in those days before I ever did.

One day in Apache, I saw everybody around there drinking. I was about the last one to start home after the others had gone. As I started back, I saw someone coming up behind me. I thought I would ride up fast to him and go on to camp with him. I caught up to him and recognized him. He reached over and grabbed my bridle reins. He said, "Grandson,[3] do you drink?" I told him "No." He said, "Here is a half a pint. Drink it all. If you don't drink it, I'm going to shoot you through the stomach." The first thing I thought about was that this fellow had cut his wife up with a knife once. It scared me. I said, "Give it to me." I started drinking it. It sure was strong. I drank the whole thing up. While I was drinking it, we were riding along and he was still holding my reins. I thought that it was all gone. When we reached the creek, he stopped my horse. He reached down and pulled out another half pint. I drank it down. This time it didn't burn my throat so badly. The other fellow said, "That's good." We rode along. This time when we stopped, he pulled out a whole pint. He said, "You drink half, and I'll drink half." I saw just a few bubbles, and already his half was gone. He just grunted when he finished. After I drank my share up, everything began looking different. I wasn't afraid of anything. I felt good. I reached over and switched his horse across the face. When we got close to camp, he took out another bottle. I don't remember how much it was. After that I must have got off my horse, and it must have run off and left me. I don't know how I got back to camp. Maybe some fellow came out in a buggy and got me.

[3] Calling someone much younger than oneself by the grandchild term, and an elder by the grandparent term, was a mode of establishing a relationship of warmth and familiarity. The Kiowa Apache use the same term in their language to address grandparent and grandchild.

Next day I was sick. I wanted to drink a lot of water. I can't remember much more because I was too drunk. My wife got after that old man I was with for getting me drunk.

A couple of weeks later I was at Anadarko. There was a saloon there called "Owl Saloon." I thought about getting a drink, so I went over there alone. They were gambling in the back part of the place. Some of the older people that had been drinking saw me come in. Sidney Hall asked if I wanted a drink. They had buckets of beer then. He ordered me a gallon bucket of beer. I said, "This doesn't taste like what I've drunk. It isn't as strong." We both sat there and drank it up. That was really beer. It wasn't like this 3.2 beer.[4] He asked if I wanted more. He told me to go ahead and buy it. I said I wanted something stronger. I bought a pint for fifty cents. We both drank it up. While we were drinking, Alonzo Redbird came in. He liked to drink. He called to me, "Brother, you like to drink?" He was feeling pretty good. Alonzo bought a bottle, and we sat down and drank it. I began to feel it. I was getting dizzy. I don't know how I went out of the saloon. I don't know who took me to camp. That was the second time. All those fellows I used to drink with have quit since. I'm the only one left who still drinks. My wife didn't mind it too much then. After this, I got to drinking every now and then. I was really getting started at it. I would drink every week. I had good horses and a good home then. I had everything. I started gambling and running around with other women. Every time I went out drinking after that, my wife would run off somewhere.

One day she told me, "We are going to have to quit. I'm not going to come back to you any more." The worst part of this was in 1923 and 1924, when we began to fight and have trouble. I told her that the next time she ran off we would be through for good. When she ran off again, I was staying home with my children. I went to the agent and told him that my wife and I were having trouble and that I wanted a paper to quit her. I told him that I wanted to keep my children. The agent told me, "All right. We will take care of it. You can keep your children. I know you are a good worker, but I know you like to drink." The agent called us together. Big Joe was a policeman then, and he brought Louisa in. The agent told her that she would have to give some of our eldest daughter's land to our

---

[4] When Jim Whitewolf's autobiography was recorded, 3.2 per cent alcoholic content was the legal limit in Oklahoma.

daughter Eliza. He said otherwise he would have her put in jail for six months. We agreed on that, so they gave us a divorce. I told her to go ahead and get married whenever she wanted. I said, "We are both free. Do what you want." Even today, though, she comes to visit and talk with me. She still treats the children well. This was 1925, when we got the divorce.

After that I ran around with women a lot, but I never did get married again. My mother told me, "Don't marry again." She said that any new wife wouldn't treat my children right and we would have trouble again.

I worked here and there after that. I worked on different Indian projects. I had one job killing prairie dogs. I did some farming, too. Then later I had an operation. My eyes began to go bad, so I quit working regularly. But up to this day I always make a big garden every year. I plant about an acre. I plant mostly watermelons and tomatoes and also some beans, potatoes, and onions. It's just for my own use at home.

JUST BEFORE Louisa and I were divorced, a field matron named Miss Brennan went with her to the Agency to see about our children. The children were staying with me at the time. They told the Agency that I agreed to let her take them for five months. They said I was drinking and should give up some of my land for the children.

Louisa took the children. She was staying with Colonel. Before the five months were up I heard she left them. I went after them and brought them to my home. When Louisa returned and found them gone she went to Miss Brennan and reported on me. Miss Brennan came down to my place and took the children back. Not long afterward, Louisa left the children again and went off to a Kiowa dance at Clinton. She left my children over at Alonzo Redbird's place. Alonzo was blind. My father went to the Agency and reported it. They gave my father the papers on the children and told him not to let Miss Brennan have them again if she came around. The Agency took away Louisa's five months' custody of the children. Miss Brennan came down to my place alone, and she was mad. My father was mad about having his grandchildren mistreated like that, too. When she asked for me, my father said I was away and would be back that evening. She asked for the children. My father blew up and told her to get out. He said, "God damn it, get out of here! You are helping a crazy woman make trouble." She went back and reported to the Agency. They told her to get Louisa and me to come there to talk it over. Then we got divorced.

That Miss Brennan was a troublemaker. She was a white woman who dressed up like an Indian. She wore a shawl and moccasins. Whenever Louisa came to her and told lies about me, she would jump in her car and come down to make trouble.

IT WAS after I broke up with my wife that my mother got sick. She was always vomiting up something dark-looking. When she got worse, my boy took her to the hospital. By this time there were no more Indian doctors. The hospital doctors examined her and said that we had come too late. They said that even if they did operate on her, she couldn't live because she was too old. She was about eighty, I think. They brought her back home. She was pretty sick, but she could talk all right and she knew what she was talking about. She knew that she wasn't going to live. She told me, "When I am gone, you can have this home and live here with your children. I have made my will that way. I am giving your father forty acres.[5] I have told him that before he dies he is to give it back to you." We kept trying to help her. We called in different town doctors, but they said she was too far gone. One day I was outside, when someone came out and told me my mother wanted to talk with me. I went into her room. She told me that she was going to leave me, maybe this same day or that night or the next day. She said she was tired. I sat beside her. She brushed my hair. She said, "Even when you were small, I used to do this for you. After I leave you, I don't know how you will live or what you will do." When she got through, she lay back down, and I thought from the way she was acting that she might be getting better. It was about four o'clock that afternoon when she passed away. That was about all of it. I can remember that when I was small my mother never got after me. She never whipped me.

After her death, my father came over near Fort Cobb to stay. After that my father was sick. One day I had to make a lease down near Cyril. I wasn't gone two days when I heard that my father had

---

[5] Property at this time was individually owned; the former reservation was allotted in severalty at the turn of the present century. See Introduction, pp. 15–16.

died. My mother liked me best. My father never thought too well of me. It was about two or three years after my mother's death that my father died.

Now I have things fixed so that my son Ben's daughter can have that land. I have my other land all fixed so that my children and grandchildren will get it after me. I bought a car for my son Ben and gave it to him.

Sometime before the First World War the first trouble began with my wife. She never went around to the dances before that. She was kind of a Christian woman.[6] I was farming then.

Then there was a big dance at Colonel's. There was an old woman there, Louisa's aunt, who talked to her there. She asked Louisa why she had to go home early. She told Louisa I was making a slave of her and keeping her home working. Several times after that she talked to Louisa against me and told her to go to the dances. Then Louisa started going around and taking part in them. She lost interest in our house and farm. Since our separation Louisa has been married several times. Now she is married to a Comanche man and lives at Lawton. After that I never got married again. They always used to say that a stepmother never took good care of step-children. My mother told me to stay single.

---

[6] The association of abstinence from Indian dances with being a "Christian woman" is a missionary-inspired one. Persistent efforts were made by Christian missionaries to discourage their converts from participation in native ceremonies.

V

Religions, Old and New[1]

LONG AGO, a fellow was out seeking a vision. He stayed out three or four days. Then Owl spoke to him: "What are you looking for? What do you want?" He said, "The other people have medicine and that is why I am here. I want to learn something." Owl said, "I can give you something. Tie some sinew around each finger. Put up a tipi and sit on the west side. Hang a cloth down in front of you from above. Have a pipe there. Sing this song that I will teach you. Then I will do anything you want." Owl taught him this song. Then Owl said, "Go back to your camp. I will talk to you in your sleep."

The man returned to camp. His grandfather asked, "Why do you go out there like that? You have no medicine. You don't have anything." The man said, "I do know something. When anybody gets sick I will cure them."

The old man told the others that his grandson could doctor and that he could tell them anything they wanted to know.

In the spring the buffalo were getting scarce and the people were running out of food. They told the old man to call his grandson in to help them. The old man went to him and told him about it. He asked the boy to find out where they could get buffalo. The boy said the people should gather together and he would come and tell them what to do. He told them to have a pipe there.

The people fixed up a place and got ready. The man came and smoked with them. Then he put down the pipe. He told the people what they would have to do to get his help. He said they had to put up a tipi, with a cloth hanging down on the west side, and to bring a pipe. They were all to come and sit in the tipi with him. They had to tie sinew on his fingers, toes, and tie his hands and his legs together

---

[1] The vision quest, characteristic of Plains Indian religions, was practiced among the Kiowa Apache, but probably to a lesser degree than among other tribes of the area. The production of voices by shamans through ventriloquism, the hallucinatory hearing of voices by audiences at rituals, and the performance of various sleight-of-hand tricks were common elements.

with sinew. He said that he had already taught his grandfather the song he had to sing.

The people did everything that he told them. There was a fire burning in the tipi. The man went behind the cloth and sat down. His grandfather had a buffalo-hoof rattle. The boy told his grandfather to sing, and also to let the fire die down and remove the wood from it, so it would be dark.

The old man sang. On the second round of singing, the tipi began to shake, as if a big wind were hitting the top of it. The noise got louder and louder. It sounded like the rattle he was shaking. It came down from the top of the tipi. Then the man said everybody should be very quiet and listen. When the noise reached the ground, inside the tipi, it sounded like a crying baby. The boy said, "Do not cry that way." It cried all the louder Twice more he asked it not to cry, and it cried louder. Then the boy said, "Cry all you want to." The voice stopped crying. Then the boy knew that the voice must be of the Klintidie. The voice spoke. It sounded like it was talking through its nose, and no one except the boy could understand what it said. It said, "I am crying for my little brother. I am the one who went west on the warpath and got killed. I cry because I am sorry for my little brother." The voice called out its own name and said, "That is my name. I was killed only a little while back, so I will return and send you one of the others who will tell you what you want to know; one who knows more than I do." Then the tipi began to shake again and the voice left.

The boy asked his grandfather to sing two songs again and to stop when the voice returned. On the second song the shaking began and the voice entered and came down to the ground. The old man stopped his songs. The voice asked the boy why he called. The boy said his people were hungry and wanted to know where meat could be found. The voice said, "When I leave here I will go a long way. It will be cold, for four days. The buffalo will follow the cold weather. On the fourth night the buffalo will pass by here. That night it will not be cold, but snow will be falling. Be ready for them." Then the voice asked if that was all they wanted to know. The boy said "Yes." Then the boy asked the voice to smoke before departing. As they were sitting there they could see the light in the pipe and it sounded like somebody was handling it. They heard a sucking noise on the pipe. Then they heard the shaking noise again and soon everything got quiet.

Then the boy told them to kindle the fire again and make it bright inside the tipi. Then the boy said to remove the cloth in front of him. He was no longer tied up. All the sinew was piled on one side of him. He told his grandfather to fill the pipe and pass it. When they were all through smoking, the boy said he would tell them about what he had been told.

The boy spoke, "The first one you heard who was crying was someone who was killed when he was fighting. There are going to be four days of cold weather. On the fourth day it will be warmer and snowing. Then the buffalo will come close by. Be ready. Sharpen your knives. Cut lots of wood."

On the fourth morning, the boy's grandfather got up early and saw a herd of buffalo. He called the people to come and kill them.

WHEN OUR people had the Sun Dance, it was done together with the Kiowas. The Kiowas sent some people to find a place to have it, somewhere near a lot of cottonwood trees. When that place was found, the Kiowas and Apaches together would move toward it, a day at a time, so they would arrive at the place on the fourth day. Once they arrived at the place for the dance, no one was permitted to hunt or to butcher. If they did, someone from the Manitidie or Klintidie would catch him, kill his horse, and whip him. They were like soldier-police, watching things. If anyone really needed to go hunt, he had to give a smoke to them and get permission to go.

On the four-day trip to the place of the Sun Dance, if a dog crossed the path of the Manitidie, they would shoot it and drag it to the Sun Dance place. Then the women would cook it, and all of them had to eat some, whether they liked it or not. Just before the Manitidie reached the Sun Dance place, they would start to shoot arrows into the air and dance and sing. If an arrow accidentally came down and killed or hurt someone, nobody did anything about it. If the Manitidie brought in a dog that crossed their path, they all went to a special tipi where they ate it. Then the Manitidie did their part of the work to prepare for the Sun Dance. They helped cut down brush and bring it in. The women brought in sand and dirt to fix up the Sun Dance place.

One time a Kiowa man ran off and hunted buffalo while the people were on their way to the Sun Dance place. Some of the Kiowa Gourd Dancer group went after him. They caught him. He got off his horse and sat down. They came up, whipped him, and threw away his meat. He sat there and took the beating, because he knew he had disobeyed the rules of the Sun Dance. If he had gotten up and tried to strike back, they could have killed him right there. There was this rule against killing animals during the Sun Dance, but I never heard anything about what might happen if the rule were broken, or any reason they gave for having the rule.

I heard that the day after they whipped that man, the Gourd Dancers called a meeting. There were two women in the Gourd Dance group who were leaders. They were going to talk about the man that they whipped. The men told the two women, "We are all going to bring gifts to the man we whipped. Bring everything right here and we will put everything together."

There were two men in the group who had whips. They went to the man's camp and told him he was wanted. They brought him over to the group and sat him down. Meantime the Gourd Dance group was dancing and singing. Then they quit dancing and singing when he got there. The two women leaders and the two men with the whips had to give gifts to the man first. Then all the members gave him presents. They could give him anything they thought he could use. One of the women gave him a horse; the other gave him a mule. The men gave him horses, buckskin and beads.

The rule was that when someone was whipped like that for doing wrong during the Sun Dance, if he took it without fighting back, he would be given gifts and forgiven. But if he fought back he might even be killed. If they didn't kill him for fighting back, they wouldn't give him anything. Some of the people might have broken the rules just so they would get a lot of horses and things given to them. This man was one who knew the rules well. He probably broke them on purpose, to get presents.

ONE TIME, before the country opened, the Apaches were camping east of Two Hatchet Creek. Some Cheyennes camped just to the east of there. After several nights, the Cheyennes came over and said they wanted to play the Apaches a hand game. The Apaches got everything ready.

The next day the Cheyennes had everything ready and knew what they were going to bet. The Apaches were good at switching the bone from one hand to the other without anyone being able to see it. That is why they could beat everybody in the hand game.

In the evening the Cheyennes came to the Apache camp. They were singing. When all of them got there they sat down. Everything was ready. There were four sticks in the middle and four on each side. One of the Cheyennes who was noted as a good player brought a rib and put it down on the ground in front of himself. Then they began betting. Everything was put up—horses, blankets, saddles and bridles. They agreed they were going to play just one game.

One old Apache man said, "We are betting a lot of things. We have played this game many times. But this Cheyenne man here must know something, the way he has placed that rib there. You had better go get Daveko to help us."

The fellows who went after Daveko told him, "We are playing those Cheyennes and betting heavily. You better come over and help us out."

Daveko said, "Yes, I already know about it." He went with them and sat right opposite the Cheyenne who had put the rib down on the ground.

They got started. They began singing the handgame songs. The Cheyenne man said, "You go ahead and hide it first and I will guess."

Daveko said, "No, you hide it first and I will guess." So the Cheyenne man hid the bone first. Daveko said, "I can tell which hand he has it in. I can see it." But when he guessed, the Cheyenne had it in the other hand and Daveko lost that time.

Then Daveko hid the bone and the Cheyenne missed when he guessed. Right then both of them knew that each was using some kind of power against the other.

It was the Cheyenne's turn to hide the bone. When Daveko guessed, he reached over with his opposite hand as if he were pulling on someone's nose and produced the bone, showing Daveko to be wrong. So when it was Daveko's turn to hide the bone again, he did the same thing.

The third time, the Cheyenne pulled his hand down from up in the air and produced the bone, making Daveko wrong again. So when Daveko hid the bone again, he reached with the opposite hand as if to draw the bone out of the fire, and showed it to the Cheyenne.

The people were beginning to get tired of singing all this time. When the Cheyenne hid the bone again and Daveko guessed, he made a motion with his other hand toward the Apaches across from him, and showed them the bone.

On Daveko's fourth turn at hiding the bone, instead of putting his hands behind him, he showed the Cheyenne the bone in his right hand, then closed his fists. When the Cheyenne guessed, the bone wasn't there. Daveko reached over toward the rib that the Cheyenne had put on the ground, and picked up the bone. It was the Cheyenne's turn to hide the bone once more, but he suspected what Daveko was going to do next. He said everybody was tired and the game should stop. Daveko told him, "Go ahead and hide it again. Whenever your power or my power runs out, one side will win. We are going to sit here until we use up our powers."

The Cheyennes began talking among themselves. They said, "We have already lost. Our man has refused to hide the bone again. He knows the other man has more power." So the Apaches got all the stuff that the Cheyennes had bet.

WHEN I WAS in school I had a good friend named Claude. He was a Comanche boy. I played marbles with him and he always gave me fruit and things his father brought him. We shared things like that. Once he got sick and went home. Later he died. Two or three years after that his father sent Henry Brownbear for me. He gave me a good horse, a saddle, and bridle that he had intended for his own boy. I was just like his own son.

After some time he came to me. He said, "I have a good medicine for stomach-ache. I learned it myself. Coyote gave me the power for it. I am going to give it to you." He took me out and showed me a certain root. He dug some up. He showed me how to boil it. He told me to smoke and pray before using it. Then I was supposed to give it to the sick person to drink in the morning and afternoon. He said not to tell people all about it. I do not know the name of the root.

One time my boy Ben had stomach-ache. Rob Curtis couldn't cure him and neither could the white doctor. I decided to try my medicine. I dug the roots and prepared the medicine for Ben. I prayed, "I do not know who created this medicine, but I want you to help me." Ben drank some of it in the morning and again in the afternoon. In three or four days he got well.

A person who was cured by that kind of a medicine might come to you when you are old and say, "You are getting old. I would like to learn your medicine." He would give you a cigarette when he made the request. It would be hard to turn him down, and usually they agreed to teach that person. It wasn't necessary to consult any power about it. If you thought the person was crazy and would not take care of the medicine, you would try to make an excuse. You might say you had already promised the medicine to somebody else.

AROUND 1897, when the government was building homes for us, they were building one for Baca-ay. He was a powerful medicine man. He asked Sidney Hall and me to haul the lumber for his house. Sidney had just bought a horse at this time. Sidney was Baca-ay's cousin. He asked Sidney to give him the horse. Sidney told him, "I just bought it and I want to keep it a while. Later I will give it to you." The old man didn't like that. He said, "I thought you are my cousin. That is why I asked for the horse." Sidney said, "This evening we will get your lumber and take it over where you are going to build."

We went to town and got the lumber. We planned to deliver it the next day, to his place four miles west of Stecker. We were driving along, and got to within a half mile of the place, when Sidney's chest began to hurt. He asked me to drive. Sidney lay down and felt pretty sick. When we got there I unloaded all the lumber. I fixed a place for Sidney to lie down while I worked. Then I fixed him a place to sleep in the wagon on the way back. He said, "I may die on the way." I drove fast. Sidney told me to hurry. We got back to Anadarko about sundown and they carried him out of the wagon wrapped in a quilt. That night they called two Comanche medicine men to doctor him. They didn't do much good. The next day Sidney's sister said they would have a peyote[2] meeting and call in more

---

[2] In the form in which it is eaten in peyote meetings, peyote consists of the dried tops of a small cactus (*Lophophora williamsii*) which grows in the Rio Grande region of the United States and Mexico. Its physiological and psychological effects sometimes include nausea, muscular relaxation, color visions and a generalized feeling of well-being. It has long been debated—frequently in an emotional, partisan manner—whether peyote is an addictive drug. My view is that, among Indians who use it for religious purposes, it is not. Kiowa Apache traditions have it that they learned about peyote from one Nayokogal, who was either a Mescalero or Lipan Apache from New Mexico. La Barre, in his definitive work *The Peyote Cult* (Yale University Publications in Anthropology, No. 19, 1938), credits the Kiowa Indians with first using peyote about 1880; the close association of the Kiowa and Kiowa Apache would make it likely that the same date would hold for the latter tribe. The formal organization of the peyote

doctors. Alonzo and I helped put up a big tipi. All that time they were doctoring Sidney. Later in the day he became delirious and didn't know anything. Just before the meeting began, the Comanche who was to run it asked another man to build the fire. He told them to bring Sidney to the tipi after the meeting started. The peyote chief gave Sidney some peyote. It took him a long time to swallow it. At midnight they prayed for him. After the water was taken out of the tipi, the chief called on Henry Brownbear, a Comanche, to doctor Sidney. When he got through sucking on him, they asked Sidney how he felt. He said it still hurt. Then Comanche Jack tried, and Sidney still was in pain. The peyote chief tried, and it did no good. He chewed some peyote and gave it to Sidney. Then one of the Comanche doctors spoke to another man there and told him they couldn't do Sidney any good. He rolled a cigarette for the man. The old man said he would help. He smoked and gave a short prayer. He sucked on Sidney's chest, fanned him, and smoked him with cedar. When they asked Sidney how he felt, he said the pain was still very bad. The old man sat down and prayed and smoked again. He said he would sit and try to think what to do to help Sidney. He was a very strong medicine man. Toward daylight he spoke to the chief, "Here is what I have learned from my power. I am to quit here in the morning. Someone will come who is all dressed up. You will know by the way he is dressed that he has power. This man here is not sick. He has been witched. The man who is coming has the power to cure him." When he finished, the peyote drum[3] went around. When morning came and they had eaten, they carried Sidney out, wrapped in the blanket.

We were all seated outside. Then we saw a man coming from the north leading a white horse. When he got close we could see he was an Apache medicine man. It was Baca-ay. He tied up his horse. Henry Brownbear had a cigarette all ready. Baca-ay came up and

---

religion as a church occurred in 1918, when "in response to suggestions made by James Mooney, an early student of the peyote cult, the Indians of this area formed the 'Native American Church,' together with other Indian groups in Oklahoma, and obtained a charter under Oklahoma state laws." (Charles S. Brant, "Peyotism Among the Kiowa-Apache and Neighboring Tribes," *Southwestern Journal of Anthropology*, 6: 2 [1950], 220.)

[3] The peyote drum is made of a heavy iron kettle, half filled with water, with a soaked piece of buckskin stretched across the top and tightly tied in place.

said, "Hello, brother. I sure want a smoke." Henry turned and lit the cigarette; then he handed it to him. Baca-ay looked at the cigarette and asked, "Why did you give me this one?" Henry said, "You wanted to smoke. Go ahead." Baca-ay smoked it a little bit. Henry said, "Now you see that last night we had a meeting and prayed to our Father and his Son for our brother here to get well. You know that when anyone gives you a smoke, you have to follow the rule and help. We want you to doctor him. If you break the rule and refuse, it will all turn back on you."[4] Baca-ay wore a feather and had markings on his face that represented his medicine. He started sucking on Sidney's chest and blew into the air. Sidney was still in pain. He did it a second time but it didn't help. Henry Brownbear said, "Keep trying. You know what's wrong with him." Then Baca-ay said to fix up a tent and take Sidney inside. Alonzo and I went to tell the people to fix the tent. They carried Sidney in. They asked Alonzo and me to sit on either side of him. I was interpreting for Baca-ay because Henry Brownbear couldn't understand Apache. I brought in some coals and Baca-ay's medicine bag. He took some medicine and put it in the fire, and then he smoked some feathers in the fire. They had Alonzo and me hold Sidney up and brace him. Baca-ay rubbed his hand on the ground, drew it across his mouth, and sucked on Sidney's chest. The second time he sucked, he thought he had something.[5] He went to the door and blew it out of his mouth. He then took his feathers and began to fan Sidney. Sidney stretched, and when Henry Brownbear asked how he felt, he said he was all right.

That was the way of the old people. Because Sidney had turned Baca-ay down, he witched him.[6] Sidney got well all at once. It was that way when you were witched. If you were just sick, you would get well gradually.

MY FATHER was in New Mexico once for five years. That was before I went to school. He was there with another man. His friend told

---

[4] That is, supernatural power will turn against its holder.

[5] After sucking the painful part of the body, shamans commonly produced an object by sleight-of-hand, declaring it to be the cause of the illness. The psychosomatic value of this kind of treatment might be compared to improvement in the patients of modern physicians who are given placebos for psychogenic complaints.

[6] Vague, unspecific malaise was often attributed to witchcraft, particularly if one had reason to feel that another harbored a grievance against him.

him to watch out for a certain kind of woman at Mescalero that wore beads in a certain way. I don't know just what way it was, but they said that kind of woman had power to catch men, even though they were often ugly women. They could witch if you turned them down, too. My father went to a dance where there was a woman like that. He and his friend were just looking on. She spoke to them, "Hello, wet-foot Apaches. Do you boys want some women?" My father's friend said, "No, we don't want any women." She got kind of mad and walked away. She said, "All right, you will find out some of these days." My father told his friend, "You shouldn't have talked to her."

Several days later they started home. When they got here, my father's friend went crazy. He would go around with his hair uncombed and act funny. We were camping near where Harry Sunchild lives. He wandered off and came back with a live rattlesnake around his neck, like beads. His wife and his sister were scared. "This is my pet," he said. In a few days he got sick. He wouldn't eat. He was out of his head and didn't know anything. After a while he died.

Before long my father began to wander off by himself, two days at a time, in the woods. He was going crazy. Some of the men caught him and tied him up. They hid knives from him for fear he might kill his own children.

My father's sister went to Saddleblanket and gave him a cigarette and offered him a horse. Saddleblanket's way was to doctor for anything people could afford to offer him. We put up a tipi at our place for Saddleblanket to use in doctoring my father. Twice a day he doctored him. At night they tied him up. I don't know how many days he doctored. Then Saddleblanket told my sister, "I have tried hard and he is only a little better. I will try one more way." They put up a peyote meeting. In the morning, Saddleblanket told my father he would take him to the creek to doctor him. He told him to dive down and get some sand and rub it on himself. Then Saddleblanket made him sit out in the sun. His back felt like it was going to burn up. Then he suddenly heard thunder. Saddleblanket said, "When it rains it will cool you off and you will get well." My father stayed there in the rain and then he was better. He told me, "Watch out for that kind of woman if you ever go down to New Mexico. They are crazy."

SOMETIME between 1901 and 1903, when my first child was born, I went to the "Owl Poor" bundle[7] to pray. Apache John had it then. I told my wife, "Tomorrow we will go to Apache John's. We lost our first child, but now we have one. We will cover the bundle with a cloth, and pray to it." At that time I didn't believe in the white man's ways; I believed in the Indian way.

The next day we left early for Apache John's place. He was sitting under his arbor. When he saw me carrying a cloth he knew what I had come for. He said the bundle was in the tipi. He went into the tipi to prepare things. His wife told us when he was ready. I took the baby inside by myself. The medicine bundle was tied to a tipi pole. John told me to pray. He said, "This bundle was given to the Apache by our Father and he will know through the prayer what you want." When I finished praying I covered the medicine bundle with the cloth. Then John told me to bring my wife inside. I left the baby with his wife, and brought my wife inside the tipi. We sat down. Apache John said, "It is good that you have come here to believe as the old people believe. It has been this way since long before my time. On the outside there are many ways that you can take. There is the white man's way and there is the peyote way. All of these ways were made by God, so that you may pray for your children to grow well and that you may live to have the things you want. You can see these things for yourself."

I told him, "I know these things, because my mother told me about them. Now I want to ask you something. I want you to tell me about the sweathouse."

John told me to come back with my wife three days later. We ate dinner there with him and his wife, and then we went home.

When I got home I told my father about the visit to Apache John. He said it was a good thing and that I should be sure to go back again as John had requested. He said that he was not supposed to teach me about the sweathouse, but I could learn it from the old man, Apache John.

When we went back to Apache John's he began telling us that night about the sweathouse. He said that we should get up early in the morning and not drink or eat. He told us where we could find willow trees. He said that the first willow cut should fall northward, the second should fall eastward, the third should fall southward, and the

7 One of the four medicine bundles.

fourth should fall westward. He said that after those four willows were cut in that manner, the rest could be cut freely.

After I cut the willows John showed me how to place them. One bunch was laid on the ground facing northward. Then I cleaned a round patch of ground. I dug a round hole in the middle, about a foot deep. Then I cut a V-shape patch leading from the hole in each of the four directions.

The old man had a pile of bark from the cottonwood tree. There were rocks inside the pile, and he had a pitchfork to stir the rocks around inside the pile after it was lit.

He showed me how to place the four willows in the proper directional places. I bent the north and south ones over at the top and tied them; then the east and west ones. Then I started by the south willow and worked around clockwise putting in the rest of the willows. When the whole framework was up, I covered it over thickly with quilts, which would hold the steam in. On the east side there was a quilt used as a doorway. John told me to get some horse manure and put it on the west side, inside the sweathouse. Then I placed a bundle of grass on the west side of the manure. Outside, there were two fellows, already stripped and fixing themselves grass switches to use in the sweathouse.

Outside, they lit the pile of bark with the rocks inside. Then Apache John sent me for the "Owl Poor" medicine bundle. When I returned, there were two fellows lying down inside the sweathouse, facing east. Apache John sat on the west side. I put the pipe down on the grass near the horse manure, and placed the medicine bundle on his right. I brought in a coal, and Apache John put it on the ground right on top of some crumbled manure. Then he put some kind of medicine on the coal. He reached down with a forked stick and picked up a burning chip of manure and lit the pipe, which was already filled with tobacco when I brought it to him. Then he prayed and passed the pipe to one of the old men who were lying down. He smoked and passed it on to the other one, and then the pipe was returned to its place on the grass. The coal was put out.

My wife brought a bucket of water up to the sweathouse, and I brought in some red-hot rocks. I rolled them in with a pitchfork, and one of the other men guided them with a stick into the hole. I put the water on John's left.

Outside the sweathouse my wife lay down on the west side, and I lay down on the east side. When they told us, we alternated in raising up the quilts and letting air go in. Inside they used a buffalo horn to dip water and pour it on the hot rocks. I could hear the steam hissing as I lowered the side of the sweathouse. My wife and I took turns, and raised the sides four times, each time a little higher. After the fourth time, John drank water from the horn and passed it to the others, then to me, and finally I passed it to my wife. That was the first we drank since we had started.

When the men came out, their bodies were all red. I took the medicine bundle and pipe back to the tipi. Then I removed the quilts from the sweathouse but left the willows standing. The others had gone to the creek to bathe. After that we ate the food that John's wife had prepared, and then we sat around and told stories.

In the sweathouse ceremony, women are not permitted to enter at any time. But a sweathouse can be built and used by women to bathe, in a non-religious way.

There are rules about the "Owl Poor" medicine bundle. You are not supposed to beat a drum close to it, and you can't play a hand game near it. A menstruating woman cannot go near it.

The prayers in the sweathouse ceremony are addressed to Nuako-lahe, the "one who made the earth."

THERE IS a story from long ago about the origin of peyote. It goes back to the times the Indians were fighting each other. On the other side of New Mexico a group of Indians were camped, and they were attacked by other bands. The mountains there were very high. The tribe that was attacked got scattered. There was just one woman and her boy left. They were Lipan Apaches. It was very hot and dry there. All the water had dried up. They had no food or water and there was none around them.

The woman told her boy, "I am tired and hungry and thirsty. We will rest here. Maybe I will die here. You go on. If you can't find anything, maybe you will die somewhere." It was early in the morning. The boy went out in the mountains. She told him to look around to see if he could see anyone. He walked around. Then something above spoke to him. It said, "I know you are hungry. Look down ahead of you. You will see something green. Eat it." He saw a green plant and dug it up and began to eat it. He looked around and saw many more. He ate some. Soon his hunger was gone, as if he had eaten a lot of meat. He dug some more of the plants up and took them to his mother. He told her of the voice that had spoken to him. She ate some of the plants, and felt as if she had eaten a big meal of meat. Her hunger was gone.

In the middle of the afternoon it was very hot. She said, "I do not know who gave us this. I am going to pray to him." She prayed for water and to find their people again. Later on, a cloud began to darken the sky and it thundered. Rain fell and there was water running through the mountains. They drank and rested there that night.

During the night the woman dreamed. Someone came to her and said, "Look over there and you will see a certain mountain." She looked and saw people moving along the hills. There was a creek nearby. It was east of where she and her boy were lying. In the dream she was told to go up on a high mountain in the morning and look out, and she would see her own people. She was told to take peyote to her people and a way would be made for it.

In the morning they washed and ate some peyote. She told her son of her dream. They went to the mountain and looked out, as she had been told in her dream. She saw people settling down and camping. She knew from her dream that they would be Indians. She and her boy started toward them. One man met them. He recognized them as the lost ones. They were glad to see each other. When they reached the camp he told all the people about them.

The boy had the peyote with him. After they got settled the boy asked his mother to fix him a tipi, off by himself. He said he would go in that night and eat the peyote, and after that he would go into the mountains and lie down. He sat down inside the tipi and put the peyote on the ground, just as it looked when he first saw it. He prayed to the spirit that had shown him the peyote. "You have helped me. When I eat peyote tonight I want you to help me to find a way for it." He had a bow and arrow, and he drummed on the bowstring with the arrow. He sang two songs. He smoked a pipe made of bone from a deer's leg. He drummed and sang all night long. Early in the morning he went to the mountains and stayed there all day and night. The following morning he came back.

He did this several times. He put up a tipi and sang and drummed all night, and then went alone to the mountains.

Soon the men began to talk among themselves. They said, "That young man is doing something." One time one old man went over to the boy's tipi. He called him and asked, "Are you afraid for me to come in? I want to come in." The boy told him to enter, and the old man sat down beside him. The boy gave him the pipe and he lit it from the fire. Then the boy gave him peyote to eat.

Early in the morning they went to the mountains and returned to camp just before dark. His mother had taken the tipi down in the meantime.

After that, people asked the old man what had happened. They said they were all going into the tipi next time.

Not long afterward the boy put up the tipi again. The old man came. Another man came by and asked to enter. He was told to enter clockwise and to attend to the fire. The next morning the three of them went to the mountains and stayed until sundown. The boy's mother took the tipi down.

The next day the boy told them he was running short of peyote and would go for more. He went where it was growing and brought back more of it.

The next time they put up a tipi and had a meeting a fourth man came. They told him to sit on the south side. Next day they all went to the mountains, as before. That man asked if others could come, and he was told they were welcome.

When there was a meeting again, all those men came and seated themselves, beginning on the south side and on around the tipi. As meeting after meeting took place, more men came, until the tipi was full.

All the time the boy wondered about improving the sound of his bow and arrow. He cut a long stick and thought, "I will use this to pray with, so that when I grow old I can use it to walk with." He took a horn and put stones in it to make a rattle. At the next meeting he used those things. As he held the staff and shook the horn, he sang some songs he had made.

Then he found a container of wood, already formed. He put water in it and tied a hide over it. He made a drumstick from a yucca stalk. At the next meeting he gave the drum to the man next to him, to drum for him while he sang. In the morning he told the man next to him to untie the drum. He said, "Maybe because of this horn we will get meat. The sound of this drum reminds me of the thunder I heard, and the water in it reminds me of the rain that came. Think of things that will be good to have here." The others learned songs of their own, and soon everything began to fit right in the meetings. Different ones added new things. The rocks on the drum were to represent tipi poles; the rope represented the rope holding the tipi poles at the top.

Later, Nayokogal learned of peyote and brought it to us. In time it went north into the Dakotas. To this day it is our religion. Even today different men add things to make it better. The boy told them long ago to think of things to add to make it better. Nowadays it is held on holidays like Thanksgiving and Easter, and the feast has been added to it.

ABOUT 1896 I saw a tipi west of Anadarko. I heard that they were going to have a peyote meeting there that night. There I saw my cousin, my mother's brother's boy. His name was Carl. We went in and sat down on the south side. Then they passed around the tobacco; it was Bull Durham. At the time they were smoking, the chief was the only one to pray. The Indians there were Kiowa Apaches. This place was the campground where the Indians camped in Anadarko. It was Old Man Allen's meeting. It was near the Catholic Mission, just south of the airport that is there today. That was where we got the beef rations. It was the first time I ever took part in a peyote meeting. They had peyote before this time, though.

After the smoking was over, sage was passed around. Each person would take some of it and smell it and rub himself all over with it. They did it so they would not get sickness and so they would always be strong. After the sage went around they passed the peyote around in a sack, and each one took two as it came to them and ate them. Next, the peyote chief took a bag of dried, crumbled cedar and put some in the fire. This is done because when the smoke rises up out of the fire from the cedar in it, the prayer will go out. Everyone reached out to the fire and rubbed his body with the smoke. The chief took his gourd and his staff and made a motion toward the fire four times. The drummer took his drum and drumstick and made the same motions as the chief did. Then the chief sang and the ceremony began. Each person in turn sang four songs until everyone had sung. Each one took the drum after he sang his four songs. When the chief thought it was midnight he sang one song known as the water song, *kobizi*. When he finished that song the fire chief went out after the water. He put the water right in front of the fireplace. Just after the water was brought in the peyote chief gave cedar to some member in the tipi, to pray. Then this man put the cedar into the fire. Then the tobacco was passed to the fire chief and he rolled a cigarette of corn shuck. He prayed and gave the cigarette to the drum chief. When the drum chief finished praying with this cigarette, he gave it to the peyote chief. When the chief finished praying with the cigarette, he laid it down on the floor, right in front of the representation of the moon, which is made of dirt heaped up before the fire. Then they passed the water around from the door and everyone drank. The fire chief took the water outside again. Then the drum was passed around again and the whole thing was repeated.

I sat in and watched all of this. When I ate the peyote I thought it was a wonderful thing. I felt good and listened to the songs and the prayers. They said that this was the way they prayed and that they learned it a long time ago.

When it was getting light outside and they saw morning was coming, the chief again called for water. This time he picked up a whistle that he blew four times, and then he sang the morning water song. After that the chief's wife brought in the water. Just like at midnight, they gave cedar to someone who prayed and everyone rubbed himself with the smoke. The tobacco was passed to the chief's wife and she rolled her own cigarette. Then the fire chief took a stick that is used specially for lighting the tobacco and gave her a light for her cigarette. Then she passed the cigarette around and they did the same thing as at midnight. The water went all the way around and the chief's wife was the last one to take a drink of it. She left the bucket by the fire and circled around the tipi. Then she took the bucket and went out of the tipi. When she returned with the food, they stopped singing and just continued to pass the drum on around until it got back to the chief, and then he sang four songs. The last song of the four was the final song of the night. Then the food was brought in. The chief asked someone to say a blessing for the food. After the prayer for food, the drum chief untied his drum and put his drumstick inside of it. He put the drum down in front of him. Then the chief took his gourd and staff and passed them around. Each person took the staff and held it outstretched, and shook the gourd as he said a prayer, like, "May I live to be an old man." As the gourd and staff were going around, the drum was following behind, and each one took the stick inside the drum, which had water in it, dripped the water on his hand and smeared it on his head. As each one did this he made a wish, such as, "May I become gray-haired." Following the drum they passed around the seven rocks that were underneath the thongs which held the hide over the drum. Each one rubbed himself with the rocks and made a wish, to be strong or to keep healthy. When all of these things had returned to the chief, he put them into a satchel and smoked them over the fire four times. Then the fire chief took the satchel outside of the tipi. When the fire chief returned he circled around inside the tipi before seating himself again. Then the food, in four bowls, was passed around. After everyone had eaten, the fire chief took the bowls and went out, followed by everyone in regular order. The meeting was then over. Everyone sat on the outside and told stories, and then at noon there was a big feast, after which everyone returned home.

From that day on I liked the peyote worship and even today I go to it and enjoy it. The old people said that they hoped I would learn that it was a good thing and tell the young people, so it would always go on. I believe that it is because of going to that first meeting that I have lived to be an old man today.

I REMEMBER THAT, before the country opened up, there was a Kiowa man named Joshua who went away to school. When he came back, he preached against the Indian ways. Some of the Apaches went and listened. He said that the Indian ways belonged to the devil. He preached that Christ had made everything in the world for us and that we should believe in Him. Some of the Apaches and Kiowas began to believe in it. He said to quit marrying more than one wife or we would go to hell. He preached against peyote, too. A lot of people didn't pay any attention to him. A lot of preachers came in and preached the same way. Some Indians quit using the old medicines. After Mr. Carithers left, a Mr. Adams came. He preached one time at Big Joe's place. He saw the half moon used in the peyote rite. He said, "That is what is going to take you Apaches to hell. You eat peyote and then the next day you are lazy. Cut it out." He went around asking different people if they used peyote. He told me that it was no good. He said it made my mind weak and made me crazy. He said it made me drink whisky. When he was through talking to me, I told him, "Well, I will tell you the truth. I won't argue with you. I heard what you said. You said that the Bible tells us to love each other, to tell the truth, not to hate people. Now you are talking against peyote. Have you ever used it?" He said, "No." I asked him if he ever went into the peyote tipi and heard what went on there. He said, "No." So I said, "You don't know anything about it. But you say it makes me lazy and is no good. This morning you said the Bible says to tell the truth." I asked him if he knew who planted the peyote. He said that God must have planted it because God made everything. I told him, "This peyote grows in Texas. God planted it there. I don't know how long ago it was, but the Indian found out about it. I think God made him find it and learn it was good for his body and his soul. When he found it he called people together and told them that God had given them the peyote and that it was good for them. He told them to eat it and pray all night. God gave us the peyote just like he put all the wild fruits and animals here for us. Now all the preachers talk against it. You are breaking the word of your own Bible when you tell lies about it." He never said anything to me.

Nowadays they still talk against peyote. Just like that woman on the Indian radio program the other day. I admit that about the whisky and beer she talked about. I drank it, and I know it isn't good for you. But peyote is different.

We heard of them trying to stop peyote among the Arapaho back in 1903. The Arapaho and Cheyennes used to come down and attend our meetings and tell us about the trouble up there. I heard that they sent Indian police to Arapaho meetings and that they took away their drum and gourd and turned them in to the agency at El Reno. John Fletcher, a Cheyenne, told me about this. The Indians went before the judge up there and told him that peyote was their religion and it was nothing but prayer. The judge said he had heard it was the religion of the Kiowa, Comanche, and Apache. They told him that was true and that they had learned it from those three tribes. The judge let them go.

Later on the trouble began here. The Christian people, with some Indians, went to the agent and complained about peyote. They said it made the Indians worthless and lazy. They were the same bunch that caused the trouble with the Cheyennes and Arapaho. It was two years after that when they came down here. There were three of them. The agent told us to stop using peyote down here and then it would stop among the Cheyennes and Arapaho. But he told the missionaries they would have to handle the matter between themselves and the Indians. The agent said that Quanah Parker, Apache John, and Ahpitone had explained peyote to him as their church and he didn't want to interfere. The missionaries sent a report to the Indian Office in Washington against peyote. There was no signature on the complaint when it was sent. In Washington they sent a man out to investigate peyote. That was James Mooney. He had been here before and had attended peyote meetings. They had a meeting and he attended it. A lot of the strong believers in peyote came to it. Old Man Hunting Horse was the chief of it. Mooney wrote down everything that he saw. I was at that meeting. Mooney did everything the Indians did in the meeting. He ate the food they brought in the morning, too. He came to the feast the next day. In the afternoon they spread out some blankets and sat down with Mooney to tell him what he wanted to know about peyote. They asked him what he wanted to do and what he wished to say to them. Mooney said he had come to learn about peyote and now that he had attended he would send a report to Washington on it. He said he had read many reports on peyote that were against it, but that he now believed they were wrong. He said the meeting that night was good and he hoped we would carry on this Indian religion.

He brought along four bottles of medicines that had been examined in Washington. He said that one of them contained mescal and that it was found to be intoxicating. There were two more that contained herbs that were no good. The fourth contained peyote and he said they had found nothing harmful in it.

Mooney said he was going to the Comanches and then would later attend a meeting to be given by Apache Ben. After that there would be a meeting to discuss peyote at El Reno. I went to the Comanche meeting and heard Mooney say it was good. It was the same at Ben's meeting.

At the meeting in El Reno Mooney told us to organize, choose officers, and name our church. He said we should pay two dollars a year dues and respect it as a church. He said to call it the "Native American Church."

To this day it still stands. There are still a lot of people against it, though. I don't know of any Apaches who talk against peyote, but there are some from other tribes who are against it.

We got a charter for the "Native American Church" for Oklahoma in 1918.

Lately I have heard that petitions have been sent, unsigned, to Washington, against peyote. There is going to be a meeting in El Reno soon to talk about this.

I don't like the way some people talk against peyote, but I don't have any bad feeling against them. I don't have any feeling against any church or its ways.

I REMEMBER THAT, sometime before the First World War, there was a flu epidemic. Mark Brown had gone to Little Rock, Arkansas. He was my son-in-law. He took sick down there. They sent him back here to his mother. Mark's mother came to our house and told us that Mark was sick. My daughter went back with her. She caught the flu from Mark. She was pregnant. A few nights later, they brought her back to our place. I was down by the creek playing poker, gambling, when they called me. She was lying there pretty sick. She told me that she didn't think she would live. We didn't know at that time that she had the flu. We thought that her unborn child was sick, too. We went to a neighbor's house and called Dr. Blair. He came and said that the child would be born about midnight but that it would not live. He said that if she was lucky she would live. He told us that there was this new sickness they called the flu going around and that it was awful bad. He said that he would give her some medicine so that she would give birth. He said that if it didn't help he would have to take the child out. The child was born that night; it was born dead. The doctor wasn't there when it happened. The doctor had told us to call him about nine, but the baby came before that. About three or four hours after she gave birth, she died too. She had lost too much blood. The closest funeral man was at Elgin, so I called him to come.

After the funeral, I went over to my sister's. Then Eliza became sick. She was pretty sick two days, and then I got sick, too. Stewart Williams and Alonzo Redbird came to see me while I was sick. A lot of people were sick. They told me that Frank Allen's wife and baby had died and they were going to have a funeral. A day later, Alonzo came back and said that Wilbur Allen's boy had died. When I had that sickness, I was dizzy and my throat was dry. My head ached and I had nosebleeds. The only people going around were Stewart, my boy, and Alonzo. All the other houses were quarantined. I don't know who put the quarantine on. Stewart and Alonzo would go to town to get groceries for everybody. They couldn't bring them in; they just left them by the house on the road. The doctors didn't know what to give us. It got so they didn't even come around after a while. They couldn't help. Stewart, Alonzo, and my son Ben were given some kind of medicine that protected them against the flu. They were going around digging graves for those that died. One day, Alonzo came to see me again. I knew he was coming with more bad news. He said that they were going to bury Wilbur that same afternoon of the day he died. I could hardly talk because my throat was so dry. My father felt bad that he couldn't get out to the funerals of all these men who were dying. He said that he would go anyway, even if they put him in jail for breaking the quarantine. He went out and got Clarence Staff's horses and hitched them up. My mother went, too. Just my daughter, Clarence, and I stayed there. When they had seen Wilbur, they were told that they ought to go home and take care of me and my daughter instead of going to the burial. Clarence told me before they got back, "You know the doctors can't help you. I am going to give you some peyote and some cedar. This might help." He made a sort of tea first and then the peyote tea. I gave some to my daughter, too. I drank three cups of the peyote tea. I gave my daughter a small amount of it. At night, I asked for more of the peyote tea. We drank more of it. I didn't eat anything. My headache was bad, and my nose was bleeding. Sometimes I felt as if I had lost my mind. Pretty soon I wanted to vomit. I vomited into a bucket. I told them I wanted more peyote tea. They ground peyote up and boiled it in water. We drank more of it. Then my daughter vomited. I was sick for about a week. It was on the fifth day that I started drinking the peyote tea. Before that, I hadn't taken anything. I was so weak that I could hardly walk. I felt half dead. In the evening of the fifth day, Eliza asked for food. She wanted some meat. They gave her some meat soup. I could smell it cooking, but I didn't want anything to eat. They fed her some of it and put away the rest. That night she sat up. She wanted some bread. They gave her more soup and some crackers. On the sixth day, my mother told me to eat something because it might help me. The food tasted bitter, but I ate a little bit. Later in the day I got hungry, and this time the food tasted all right to me. The soreness in my throat began to go away. On the seventh day, when they had a meal, I ate and it tasted good. The bitter taste was gone. My nose had stopped bleeding. I walked around a little. Eliza began to play. Then I thought we were getting well. By this time it was all right for the people who were getting well to visit among themselves, but no outsiders were allowed in. Clarence stayed with me a few days. Then one day he went to Big Joe's. He came back and said, "Brother-in-law, tonight they are going to have a peyote meeting there. Every-one there is sick. They want you to come." My mother told me to go there and help pray for those that were sick. She said she could take care of Eliza. Clarence asked me if I thought I could make it. I said I could. Clarence gave me some peyote that he brought back. He said, "Eat this, and sometime toward evening we will both go down there." We went down there that night and talked to Big Joe. Joe said, "We are having this meeting for those that are sick. Maybe the Lord will give us something to help us get well."

All night long we held the peyote meeting. It was sure a good one.

The next morning a doctor, a white man, came to our peyote tipi. He said, "I came here because someone called me. They said there was lots of flu here." We told him that we were having a very bad time of it and that we had prayed for help. We said, "We are glad you have come here to help us." The doctor looked around for those that needed treatment. He said that Colonel was very sick. He told us that he had a medicine that would help us get well. He doctored Colonel and the others who needed treatment badly. He left some medicine for them to take later on. Then the doctor went around to the homes where people needed attention. His medicine helped, and people began to get well. That was the first time I had seen a sickness so bad.

Long before the flu epidemic came, Apache John had said that, from all the shooting of powder and shells into the air over in Germany, poison would form in the air and some day would cause a terrible sickness. He warned us to be prepared and to pray. After the epidemic, he reminded us that he had predicted it. He said he didn't know how he knew it, but maybe something had told him. He told us to heed old people when they told us things because in the old days that was the way people learned. You remember what I told you about the old man who told all the kids to swim because he thought a sickness was coming?[8] Well, it was just like that. That is the way it is now, too. When someone who is a good man predicts something, we listen. This didn't begin recently. It has been that way from a long time back.

WHEN my mother and other old women started going to church, they were taught to say the blessing at mealtimes. One time they asked an old woman to pray. She bowed her head and prayed, "Our Father, we thank you for this food. We ask the blessing in the name of your Son. . . ." She stopped and asked another old lady the name of the son of God. The old lady told her, "Chickisha, or something like that." She said, "No. That's the place we get our rations." She couldn't think of the name, and pretty soon she just said, "It's all right, go ahead and eat."

Another time there was a white missionary woman named Miss Emma who came to our camp along the creek west of Boone. She came into camp and saw old man Allen working on a chicken house. It was Sunday, and she was going to have a prayer meeting with us under the arbor. She passed out the prayer books and gave the Sunday school lesson to the children. Allen came up with an apron on, a hammer hanging down from his side, and a saw in his hands. She said, "Hello, Allen. What are you doing?"

Allen said, "I'm working."

She said, "Today is Sunday. You aren't supposed to work today."

Allen said, "No?" and went right on working, sawing boards and hammering, right near the arbor. While he was sawing and hammering the people were singing. When the missionary woman began praying, Allen was hammering away. He hit his finger and yelled out, "God damn! Jesus!" The missionary woman stopped right there and began crying. Allen went over and spoke to her in Apache. He asked why she was crying. That woman spoke good Apache, about the only white missionary that ever did. She told him she felt bad about his swearing. The old man said he was sorry and that he wouldn't work next Sunday during church services.

One time there were five old women, my mother among them, who were getting ready to eat. They asked one of them to pray. She began, "Our Father, we are thankful for this food." Just then she heard a wagon coming up and she stopped and said, "Someone is

[8] Cf. pp. 57–58.

coming." They told her to continue her prayer but she just quit and wouldn't go on.

That same old lady was going to pray on another occasion. She told the others, "Put your heads down and close your eyes. You're not supposed to be looking around." She looked straight at one woman and said, "You! You always look around and just before I finish the prayer, you jump for the fattest meat." They put the meat down on the ground. There was a dog lying right close by them. They all closed their eyes and bowed their heads and were listening closely to the prayer. When they finished it and looked down, the meat was gone. The others were kind of angry at that woman, and she told them, "Well, you ought to look around a little bit during the prayer, just to watch the meat!"

In the early days some of the Apaches didn't like the missionaries and their work. The missionaries would go around to the camps to preach even when they knew the people there were against them. There were times that they would be preaching in those places and the men would go right on smoking and telling stories.

We didn't know the difference between Baptists, Methodists, and Presbyterians. They were all just church people to us. All except the Catholics. We knew them by their robes, and because they gave us rosaries with beads on them. The Indians said the others were no good because all they wanted was money and gave us nothing. It seems to me that the Catholics quit coming around later, but the others kept on. Maybe that is why there aren't hardly any Catholics among the Indians down here. Recently, when I was at Mescalero, New Mexico, there was an old lady who talked like our people used to. She said that Catholics were good because they gave them things, but the others made you pay for your religion. I guess the old people knew that when they prayed in the Indian way they didn't have to give anybody any money, and that was why they disliked the churches that asked for money.

Sometimes when the missionaries gave the Indians Bibles, they liked them because the paper was thin, and they could use the pages to roll cigarettes. They didn't know the Bible contained good words for them. Nowadays they have learned better.

When the Indians prayed in their own way, there was always a feast with plenty to eat. One time they heard there was going to be a Lord's Supper on Sunday. Henry Brownbear was there. They were talking about eating. The preacher was glad to see such a big turnout. When the service was over they began to serve the members of the church, who were sitting up in front. The others thought they would get to eat later on. The preacher brought some wine and small glasses and a small loaf of bread, which he served to the members. Henry was up there among them. When the bread and wine was served, he turned to his son and asked, "When are they going to feed us?" His son explained to him that there was nothing more coming. Henry jumped up and said to the people, "There isn't enough to eat here. Let's go home and eat." Everyone got up and left. That preacher just stood there.

I wasn't baptized until after I was married. All my relatives were baptized, and I was the only one who wasn't. It was in 1909 when I was baptized. East of Alden where Apache John lived was where I got baptized. There was no church there then. There was a preacher named Mr. Hicks. A lot of people were getting baptized then.

We gathered under Apache John's arbor to have our church services. I didn't go down there very much. I was always around here, getting drunk all the time. Finally they built a church down there. It was a Baptist Church. I don't know just what year it was they built it. One time Sidney Hall came to Fort Cobb to borrow some money and buy some groceries. I saw him then. I went into a saloon by the back door. Sidney Hall saw me come in. I went in and was drinking whisky. There were a lot of other Indians there. Sidney came in, and I asked if he wanted a drink. He said, "No. I used to drink but now I don't. You know I used to drink with you. When you get through drinking, come on outside and I will talk to you." Sidney and I were good friends, and we would always do things for each other. I went outside and got into my buggy. Sidney started talking to me. He said, "I know that if I ask you to quit drinking it's going to be pretty hard for you to do it. I'm going to tell you now. All of your kinfolk gather there by the church, but you are here running around drinking while your children are at home. You just think it over. Quit drinking and come to the church and work with us. Try hard to quit. This drinking is likely to hurt you. It's no good." "All right. I will go home from here. Saturday I will come down there to the church, and on Sunday I will be baptized. When you go back there, tell them what I've told you."

I started home. After supper that evening, I told my wife what

I had told Sidney. She asked me, "Do you really mean that about getting baptized, or are you just drunk? If you really mean it, I will be baptized, too."

The next morning when we were eating breakfast, my wife said, "Last night you told me that you were going to get baptized. Did you really mean it, or were you drunk then?" I told her that I really meant it. I told her that on Saturday we would get our things together and go down to the church.

When Sidney Hall got back to the church, he told his wife that I was going to get baptized that Sunday. Sidney's wife was my aunt.

My mother and father didn't know that I said I was going to be baptized. Sometime before Sunday, Sidney's wife got up and told the people that her husband told her I was going to be baptized. She said, "He is not a strong man, but he is going to join the church. I want all of you to pray for him." This was the first that my mother and father heard that I was going to be baptized. My father told my mother, "We will get up early in the morning and go see Jim. He is always drinking, and he might have been drunk when he said that. I want to find out for myself." About noon my wife said that my mother and father were coming. When they got there, my wife started preparing dinner. My mother went in to help my wife, and she asked her then, "Did Jim tell you that he was going to be baptized? That is what we heard." She told my mother that was what I said. My mother told my wife to get things ready for us to go back to the church with them that evening. I guess that they didn't want to let me get away from there. Then my mother came back into the room and spoke to my father and told him that it was true that I was going to join the church and be baptized. My father then told me to get the horses and the tents ready so that we could leave after we were through eating. Right after dinner we started out toward the church. Everybody saw me come into the church. In those days everybody in camp would help someone new put up his camp and get everything ready. That night the church bell rang. The preacher began talking. After the service he said, "All those who want to join the church and be baptized, come forward and sit down on this bench. When we sing the invocation song, those that want to come forward, do so. Anyone is welcome to do so." As they sang the song, I got up and went forward and sat down there. I listened to them sing that song. Then the preacher came to me and asked why

I came. I told him I came to be baptized. The preacher prayed for me and told me that on Sunday I would be baptized. All the members of the church formed a line and shook hands with me. I went back to camp then.

The next night they were going to have another service.

When Sunday morning came, the bell rang for church. I fixed myself up good and went into the church. I sat up on the bench in front. They told me that at ten o'clock the service would be over and everyone would go down to the creek where I would be baptized. They told Big Man to take my old clothes to the creek so that I could change into them. It was awful cold then. They told me to put on a lot of clothes, so that when I was in the water, it wouldn't soak through so quickly and make me cold. We started down to the creek. Some of the boys down there had a big fire going. On both sides of the creek bank there were lots of people. The preacher put on his hip boots. The preacher said a short prayer and started walking out into the water, and I followed him. The water was up to my hips. The preacher prayed a little while and then he ducked me backwards into the water. Then I ran back to the fire and changed my clothes. We all went back into the church again. They prayed a little while and then went back to camp. After dinner we spent the whole afternoon in church.

After that, camp broke up. On Sundays I always went back to that church. I went to church all that year. Then they made me a clerk at the church. I kept the record of when people got baptized and when they died. Whitebone was the treasurer of the church. He would keep the record of pledges to the church. Whenever anyone would pledge a beef for the church, they would butcher it in the camp and everyone got a piece of it.

Two or three months later my wife got baptized. My wife was in charge of the women's sewing meeting.

I worked at the church like that for several years. Then one time I started drinking again. This was before the First World War. My wife started going around to the dances again, and I began drinking. I began taking the old road again, drinking and running around with women. I quit my job at the church. This all led up to my wife and I quitting each other.

Epilogue

JIM WHITEWOLF'S life history, as related by him in the preceding pages, covers the period from his earliest childhood to the spring of 1949, when my ethnographic field work among the Kiowa Apache was completed and I left the region. Since it was not possible for me to return to the field to record the last years of Jim's life before he died in the mid-1950's, I have sought to reconstruct something of that period by means of information from other sources.

Despite bouts of illness and a generally deteriorating state of health which was aggravated by the toll taken over the years by alcoholism, Jim remained to the end the active, independent, strong-willed man he seems always to have been. Reluctant to be a burden to anyone, even to his closest kin, he lived alone during his last years, always near, but separately from, his children. He often walked many miles to town and to visit relatives and friends, saying that walking gave him time to think. Jim disliked to impose upon others, even to the extent of asking for rides. Only when he was without money did he turn to others for help, and in this he always felt that, even if people did not always understand, he was acting within a traditionally accepted and well understood Indian framework of values.

Jim remained the steadfast, devoted member of the Native American Church which he had been throughout his lifetime. Despite warnings of doctors about maintaining a strict diet, Jim insisted on partaking of the rich, fried foods customarily served following peyote meetings; he "had to eat these things at the meetings to be true to his church," as his son put it. And it was apparently this which brought about his death. Following a Thanksgiving peyote feast, he became acutely ill and shortly thereafter died in the hospital. His funeral was held at the Methodist Church at Boone, Oklahoma, conducted by an Indian pastor before an overflowing congregation. Jim was buried at Cache Creek Mission, near Boone.

The values of a kinship-based social system, with roles defined and ascribed on the bases of age and sex, remained close to Jim White-wolf even in his last years, when they had become largely defunct for most Kiowa Apaches. Thus Jim felt closer to his daughter than to his daughter-in-law, for Kiowa Apache ideal norms called for the maintenance of considerable reserve and social distance between parent-in-law and child-in-law of opposite sex. As his son said, in reminiscence and by way of latter-day comparison, "It's different now. I always talked to my mother-in-law. I hugged her sometimes and hauled her around and talked to her. She didn't like it at first. . . . But my father still had some of that old-time feeling. . . . My wife would speak to him, but he just couldn't bring himself to the idea."

Jim's grandchildren were closest to his heart. Frequently he went to town and spent his always scarce money to indulge them. Uppermost in his mind was the thought of leaving them something after his death. Recollections by Jim's son convey something of the warmth of Jim's relationship with his grandchildren:

> His favorite grandchild was Eliza's boy, Carlos. He called him Willy. He'd go to town and buy him apples, oranges and bananas, and see that he got the first and the last. Also he showed a little favoritism to Sally Sue's son, Johnny Lee. . . . Jim was an early riser. Johnny Lee would get up early, too—at sunrise, and go out and play. My father would see him and talk to him like a big man: "Hey you get up early. You're just like me. Someday you're going to get something from me." We heard him say that. And, sure enough, when he died he left Johnny Lee the shares from the land he'd inherited from his mother and his mother's sister. Now Johnny Lee is going through school on that money . . . every month he draws money from those shares.

One of Jim Whitewolf's most noticeable and persistent character traits was that he was always his real self, neither offering pretense to others nor indulging in self-deception as to his own nature and tendencies. For example, we know that Jim drank and got extremely drunk at times throughout his lifetime, though seldom did he directly cause trouble for others by his behavior. That others disapproved of his drinking—often rather hypocritically—annoyed him, for Jim was basically tolerant of the ways of others and expected reciprocity in this regard. On one occasion, an elderly white woman inquired, in a tone intended to be completely friendly, "Jim, why do you spend your money on whisky?" In a matter-of-fact manner—almost in the spirit of a relativistically minded ethnologist commenting on cultural differences in values—he replied, "Mrs. Brown, you spend your money on perfume; I spend my money on whisky." To those who knew him well and whom he could trust, Jim was often able to be whimsical, even a bit scornful of some of his own tendencies. On one occasion, when he had gotten drunk and was picked up by the police, causing considerable inconvenience to several people, he laughed and remarked to me, "See, I'm just like Old Man Coyote[1] in those stories I been telling you; don't listen to anybody, just go about, like crazy, get into trouble."

In the closing years of his life, Jim Whitewolf was one of a very few surviving Kiowa Apaches with considerable knowledge of the old way of life of his people, and he was often outspoken in lamenting its passage from the scene. He deplored especially the growing impersonalization of social relations, particularly among kinsmen; he was sometimes bitter in his condemnation of the devious and chicane manipulation of one person by another, which he saw as the Indians' mode of learning to adapt and survive in a sociocultural world in which they had lost all the essential controls. "Turning into a white man" was the phrase he commonly employed to refer to such behavior. In these latter regards, I suspect, Jim was, in his own way, but a symbol of the anguished protests of numberless men in all parts of the mid-twentieth-century world who look out upon vast social transformations with something less than equanimity.

[1] Coyote, the central animal character in an entire cycle of Kiowa Apache folk tales, is quite obviously a projection of human character, with its typical defects, especially irresponsibility, stubbornness, unwillingness to heed the advice of wiser heads, and he often suffers painful and ludicrous consequences.

Index

A CATALOGUE OF SELECTED DOVER BOOKS
IN ALL FIELDS OF INTEREST

A CATALOGUE OF SELECTED DOVER BOOKS
IN ALL FIELDS OF INTEREST

AMERICA'S OLD MASTERS, James T. Flexner. Four men emerged unexpectedly from provincial 18th century America to leadership in European art: Benjamin West, J. S. Copley, C. R. Peale, Gilbert Stuart. Brilliant coverage of lives and contributions. Revised, 1967 edition. 69 plates. 365pp. of text.
21806-6 Paperbound $3.00

FIRST FLOWERS OF OUR WILDERNESS: AMERICAN PAINTING, THE COLONIAL PERIOD, James T. Flexner. Painters, and regional painting traditions from earliest Colonial times up to the emergence of Copley, West and Peale Sr., Foster, Gustavus Hesselius, Feke, John Smibert and many anonymous painters in the primitive manner. Engaging presentation, with 162 illustrations. xxii + 368pp.
22180-6 Paperbound $3.50

THE LIGHT OF DISTANT SKIES: AMERICAN PAINTING, 1760-1835, James T. Flexner. The great generation of early American painters goes to Europe to learn and to teach: West, Copley, Gilbert Stuart and others. Allston, Trumbull, Morse; also contemporary American painters—primitives, derivatives, academics—who remained in America. 102 illustrations. xiii + 306pp.
22179-2 Paperbound $3.00

A HISTORY OF THE RISE AND PROGRESS OF THE ARTS OF DESIGN IN THE UNITED STATES, William Dunlap. Much the richest mine of information on early American painters, sculptors, architects, engravers, miniaturists, etc. The only source of information for scores of artists, the major primary source for many others. Unabridged reprint of rare original 1834 edition, with new introduction by James T. Flexner, and 394 new illustrations. Edited by Rita Weiss. 6⅝ x 9⅝.
21695-0, 21696-9, 21697-7 Three volumes, Paperbound $13.50

EPOCHS OF CHINESE AND JAPANESE ART, Ernest F. Fenollosa. From primitive Chinese art to the 20th century, thorough history, explanation of every important art period and form, including Japanese woodcuts; main stress on China and Japan, but Tibet, Korea also included. Still unexcelled for its detailed, rich coverage of cultural background, aesthetic elements, diffusion studies, particularly of the historical period. 2nd, 1913 edition. 242 illustrations. lii + 439pp. of text.
20364-6, 20365-4 Two volumes, Paperbound $6.00

THE GENTLE ART OF MAKING ENEMIES, James A. M. Whistler. Greatest wit of his day deflates Oscar Wilde, Ruskin, Swinburne; strikes back at inane critics, exhibitions, art journalism; aesthetics of impressionist revolution in most striking form. Highly readable classic by great painter. Reproduction of edition designed by Whistler. Introduction by Alfred Werner. xxxvi + 334pp.
21875-9 Paperbound $2.50

VISUAL ILLUSIONS: THEIR CAUSES, CHARACTERISTICS, AND APPLICATIONS, Matthew Luckiesh. Thorough description and discussion of optical illusion, geometric and perspective, particularly; size and shape distortions, illusions of color, of motion; natural illusions; use of illusion in art and magic, industry, etc. Most useful today with op art, also for classical art. Scores of effects illustrated. Introduction by William H. Ittleson. 100 illustrations. xxi + 252pp.

21530-X Paperbound $2.00

A HANDBOOK OF ANATOMY FOR ART STUDENTS, Arthur Thomson. Thorough, virtually exhaustive coverage of skeletal structure, musculature, etc. Full text, supplemented by anatomical diagrams and drawings and by photographs of undraped figures. Unique in its comparison of male and female forms, pointing out differences of contour, texture, form. 211 figures, 40 drawings, 86 photographs. xx + 459pp. 5⅜ x 8⅜.

21163-0 Paperbound $3.50

150 MASTERPIECES OF DRAWING, Selected by Anthony Toney. Full page reproductions of drawings from the early 16th to the end of the 18th century, all beautifully reproduced: Rembrandt, Michelangelo, Dürer, Fragonard, Urs, Graf, Wouwerman, many others. First-rate browsing book, model book for artists. xviii + 150pp. 8⅜ x 11¼.

21032-4 Paperbound $2.50

THE LATER WORK OF AUBREY BEARDSLEY, Aubrey Beardsley. Exotic, erotic, ironic masterpieces in full maturity: Comedy Ballet, Venus and Tannhauser, Pierrot, Lysistrata, Rape of the Lock, Savoy material, Ali Baba, Volpone, etc. This material revolutionized the art world, and is still powerful, fresh, brilliant. With *The Early Work,* all Beardsley's finest work. 174 plates, 2 in color. xiv + 176pp. 8⅛ x 11.

21817-1 Paperbound $3.00

DRAWINGS OF REMBRANDT, Rembrandt van Rijn. Complete reproduction of fabulously rare edition by Lippmann and Hofstede de Groot, completely reedited, updated, improved by Prof. Seymour Slive, Fogg Museum. Portraits, Biblical sketches, landscapes, Oriental types, nudes, episodes from classical mythology—All Rembrandt's fertile genius. Also selection of drawings by his pupils and followers. "Stunning volumes," *Saturday Review.* 550 illustrations. lxxviii + 552pp. 9⅛ x 12¼.

21485-0, 21486-9 Two volumes, Paperbound $7.00

THE DISASTERS OF WAR, Francisco Goya. One of the masterpieces of Western civilization—83 etchings that record Goya's shattering, bitter reaction to the Napoleonic war that swept through Spain after the insurrection of 1808 and to war in general. Reprint of the first edition, with three additional plates from Boston's Museum of Fine Arts. All plates facsimile size. Introduction by Philip Hofer, Fogg Museum. v + 97pp. 9⅜ x 8¼.

21872-4 Paperbound $2.00

GRAPHIC WORKS OF ODILON REDON. Largest collection of Redon's graphic works ever assembled: 172 lithographs, 28 etchings and engravings, 9 drawings. These include some of his most famous works. All the plates from *Odilon Redon: oeuvre graphique complet,* plus additional plates. New introduction and caption translations by Alfred Werner. 209 illustrations. xxvii + 209pp. 9⅛ x 12¼.

21966-8 Paperbound $4.00

DESIGN BY ACCIDENT; A BOOK OF "ACCIDENTAL EFFECTS" FOR ARTISTS AND DESIGNERS, James F. O'Brien. Create your own unique, striking, imaginative effects by "controlled accident" interaction of materials: paints and lacquers, oil and water based paints, splatter, crackling materials, shatter, similar items. Everything you do will be different; first book on this limitless art, so useful to both fine artist and commercial artist. Full instructions. 192 plates showing "accidents," 8 in color. viii + 215pp. 8⅜ x 11¼. 21942-9 Paperbound $3.50

THE BOOK OF SIGNS, Rudolf Koch. Famed German type designer draws 493 beautiful symbols: religious, mystical, alchemical, imperial, property marks, runes, etc. Remarkable fusion of traditional and modern. Good for suggestions of timelessness, smartness, modernity. Text. vi + 104pp. 6⅛ x 9¼. 20162-7 Paperbound $1.25

HISTORY OF INDIAN AND INDONESIAN ART, Ananda K. Coomaraswamy. An unabridged republication of one of the finest books by a great scholar in Eastern art. Rich in descriptive material, history, social backgrounds; Sunga reliefs, Rajput paintings, Gupta temples, Burmese frescoes, textiles, jewelry, sculpture, etc. 400 photos. viii + 423pp. 6⅜ x 9¾. 21436-2 Paperbound $4.00

PRIMITIVE ART, Franz Boas. America's foremost anthropologist surveys textiles, ceramics, woodcarving, basketry, metalwork, etc.; patterns, technology, creation of symbols, style origins. All areas of world, but very full on Northwest Coast Indians. More than 350 illustrations of baskets, boxes, totem poles, weapons, etc. 378 pp. 20025-6 Paperbound $3.00

THE GENTLEMAN AND CABINET MAKER'S DIRECTOR, Thomas Chippendale. Full reprint (third edition, 1762) of most influential furniture book of all time, by master cabinetmaker. 200 plates, illustrating chairs, sofas, mirrors, tables, cabinets, plus 24 photographs of surviving pieces. Biographical introduction by N. Bienenstock. vi + 249pp. 9⅞ x 12¾. 21601-2 Paperbound $4.00

AMERICAN ANTIQUE FURNITURE, Edgar G. Miller, Jr. The basic coverage of all American furniture before 1840. Individual chapters cover type of furniture—clocks, tables, sideboards, etc.—chronologically, with inexhaustible wealth of data. More than 2100 photographs, all identified, commented on. Essential to all early American collectors. Introduction by H. E. Keyes. vi + 1106pp. 7⅞ x 10¾. 21599-7, 21600-4 Two volumes, Paperbound $10.00

PENNSYLVANIA DUTCH AMERICAN FOLK ART, Henry J. Kauffman. 279 photos, 28 drawings of tulipware, Fraktur script, painted tinware, toys, flowered furniture, quilts, samplers, hex signs, house interiors, etc. Full descriptive text. Excellent for tourist, rewarding for designer, collector. Map. 146pp. 7⅞ x 10¾. 21205-X Paperbound $2.50

EARLY NEW ENGLAND GRAVESTONE RUBBINGS, Edmund V. Gillon, Jr. 43 photographs, 226 carefully reproduced rubbings show heavily symbolic, sometimes macabre early gravestones, up to early 19th century. Remarkable early American primitive art, occasionally strikingly beautiful; always powerful. Text. xxvi + 207pp. 8⅜ x 11¼. 21380-3 Paperbound $3.50

ALPHABETS AND ORNAMENTS, Ernst Lehner. Well-known pictorial source for decorative alphabets, script examples, cartouches, frames, decorative title pages, calligraphic initials, borders, similar material. 14th to 19th century, mostly European. Useful in almost any graphic arts designing, varied styles. 750 illustrations. 256pp. 7 x 10.   21905-4 Paperbound $4.00

PAINTING: A CREATIVE APPROACH, Norman Colquhoun. For the beginner simple guide provides an instructive approach to painting: major stumbling blocks for beginner; overcoming them, technical points; paints and pigments; oil painting; watercolor and other media and color. New section on "plastic" paints. Glossary. Formerly *Paint Your Own Pictures*. 221pp.   22000-1 Paperbound $1.75

THE ENJOYMENT AND USE OF COLOR, Walter Sargent. Explanation of the relations between colors themselves and between colors in nature and art, including hundreds of little-known facts about color values, intensities, effects of high and low illumination, complementary colors. Many practical hints for painters, references to great masters. 7 color plates, 29 illustrations. x + 274pp.
20944-X Paperbound $2.50

THE NOTEBOOKS OF LEONARDO DA VINCI, compiled and edited by Jean Paul Richter. 1566 extracts from original manuscripts reveal the full range of Leonardo's versatile genius: all his writings on painting, sculpture, architecture, anatomy, astronomy, geography, topography, physiology, mining, music, etc., in both Italian and English, with 186 plates of manuscript pages and more than 500 additional drawings. Includes studies for the Last Supper, the lost Sforza monument, and other works. Total of xlvii + 866pp. 7⅞ x 10¾.
22572-0, 22573-9 Two volumes, Paperbound $10.00

MONTGOMERY WARD CATALOGUE OF 1895. Tea gowns, yards of flannel and pillow-case lace, stereoscopes, books of gospel hymns, the New Improved Singer Sewing Machine, side saddles, milk skimmers, straight-edged razors, high-button shoes, spittoons, and on and on . . . listing some 25,000 items, practically all illustrated. Essential to the shoppers of the 1890's, it is our truest record of the spirit of the period. Unaltered reprint of Issue No. 57, Spring and Summer 1895. Introduction by Boris Emmet. Innumerable illustrations. xiii + 624pp. 8½ x 11⅝.
22377-9 Paperbound $6.95

THE CRYSTAL PALACE EXHIBITION ILLUSTRATED CATALOGUE (LONDON, 1851). One of the wonders of the modern world—the Crystal Palace Exhibition in which all the nations of the civilized world exhibited their achievements in the arts and sciences—presented in an equally important illustrated catalogue. More than 1700 items pictured with accompanying text—ceramics, textiles, cast-iron work, carpets, pianos, sleds, razors, wall-papers, billiard tables, beehives, silverware and hundreds of other artifacts—represent the focal point of Victorian culture in the Western World. Probably the largest collection of Victorian decorative art ever assembled— indispensable for antiquarians and designers. Unabridged republication of the Art-Journal Catalogue of the Great Exhibition of 1851, with all terminal essays. New introduction by John Gloag, F.S.A. xxxiv + 426pp. 9 x 12.
22503-8 Paperbound $4.50

A HISTORY OF COSTUME, Carl Köhler. Definitive history, based on surviving pieces of clothing primarily, and paintings, statues, etc. secondarily. Highly readable text, supplemented by 594 illustrations of costumes of the ancient Mediterranean peoples, Greece and Rome, the Teutonic prehistoric period; costumes of the Middle Ages, Renaissance, Baroque, 18th and 19th centuries. Clear, measured patterns are provided for many clothing articles. Approach is practical throughout. Enlarged by Emma von Sichart. 464pp.   21030-8 Paperbound $3.50

ORIENTAL RUGS, ANTIQUE AND MODERN, Walter A. Hawley. A complete and authoritative treatise on the Oriental rug—where they are made, by whom and how, designs and symbols, characteristics in detail of the six major groups, how to distinguish them and how to buy them. Detailed technical data is provided on periods, weaves, warps, wefts, textures, sides, ends and knots, although no technical background is required for an understanding. 11 color plates, 80 halftones, 4 maps. vi + 320pp. 6⅛ x 9⅛.   22366-3 Paperbound $5.00

TEN BOOKS ON ARCHITECTURE, Vitruvius. By any standards the most important book on architecture ever written. Early Roman discussion of aesthetics of building, construction methods, orders, sites, and every other aspect of architecture has inspired, instructed architecture for about 2,000 years. Stands behind Palladio, Michelangelo, Bramante, Wren, countless others. Definitive Morris H. Morgan translation. 68 illustrations. xii + 331pp.   20645-9 Paperbound $2.50

THE FOUR BOOKS OF ARCHITECTURE, Andrea Palladio. Translated into every major Western European language in the two centuries following its publication in 1570, this has been one of the most influential books in the history of architecture. Complete reprint of the 1738 Isaac Ware edition. New introduction by Adolf Placzek, Columbia Univ. 216 plates. xxii + 110pp. of text. 9½ x 12¾.
                                                   21308-0 Clothbound $10.00

STICKS AND STONES: A STUDY OF AMERICAN ARCHITECTURE AND CIVILIZATION, Lewis Mumford.One of the great classics of American cultural history. American architecture from the medieval-inspired earliest forms to the early 20th century; evolution of structure and style, and reciprocal influences on environment. 21 photographic illustrations. 238pp.   20202-X Paperbound $2.00

THE AMERICAN BUILDER'S COMPANION, Asher Benjamin. The most widely used early 19th century architectural style and source book, for colonial up into Greek Revival periods. Extensive development of geometry of carpentering, construction of sashes, frames, doors, stairs; plans and elevations of domestic and other buildings. Hundreds of thousands of houses were built according to this book, now invaluable to historians, architects, restorers, etc. 1827 edition. 59 plates. 114pp. 7⅞ x 10¾.
                                                   22236-5 Paperbound $3.00

DUTCH HOUSES IN THE HUDSON VALLEY BEFORE 1776, Helen Wilkinson Reynolds. The standard survey of the Dutch colonial house and outbuildings, with constructional features, decoration, and local history associated with individual homesteads. Introduction by Franklin D. Roosevelt. Map. 150 illustrations. 469pp. 6⅝ x 9¼.   21469-9 Paperbound $4.00

THE ARCHITECTURE OF COUNTRY HOUSES, Andrew J. Downing. Together with Vaux's *Villas and Cottages* this is the basic book for Hudson River Gothic architecture of the middle Victorian period. Full, sound discussions of general aspects of housing, architecture, style, decoration, furnishing, together with scores of detailed house plans, illustrations of specific buildings, accompanied by full text. Perhaps the most influential single American architectural book. 1850 edition. Introduction by J. Stewart Johnson. 321 figures, 34 architectural designs. xvi + 560pp.

22003-6 Paperbound $4.00

LOST EXAMPLES OF COLONIAL ARCHITECTURE, John Mead Howells. Full-page photographs of buildings that have disappeared or been so altered as to be denatured, including many designed by major early American architects. 245 plates. xvii + 248pp. 7⅞ x 10¾. 21143-6 Paperbound $3.50

DOMESTIC ARCHITECTURE OF THE AMERICAN COLONIES AND OF THE EARLY REPUBLIC, Fiske Kimball. Foremost architect and restorer of Williamsburg and Monticello covers nearly 200 homes between 1620-1825. Architectural details, construction, style features, special fixtures, floor plans, etc. Generally considered finest work in its area. 219 illustrations of houses, doorways, windows, capital mantels. xx + 314pp. 7⅞ x 10¾. 21743-4 Paperbound $4.00

EARLY AMERICAN ROOMS: 1650-1858, edited by Russell Hawes Kettell. Tour of 12 rooms, each representative of a different era in American history and each furnished, decorated, designed and occupied in the style of the era. 72 plans and elevations, 8-page color section, etc., show fabrics, wall papers, arrangements, etc. Full descriptive text. xvii + 200pp. of text. 8⅜ x 11¼.

21633-0 Paperbound $5.00

THE FITZWILLIAM VIRGINAL BOOK, edited by J. Fuller Maitland and W. B. Squire. Full modern printing of famous early 17th-century ms. volume of 300 works by Morley, Byrd, Bull, Gibbons, etc. For piano or other modern keyboard instrument; easy to read format. xxxvi + 938pp. 8⅜ x 11.

21068-5, 21069-3 Two volumes, Paperbound $10.00

KEYBOARD MUSIC, Johann Sebastian Bach. Bach Gesellschaft edition. A rich selection of Bach's masterpieces for the harpsichord: the six English Suites, six French Suites, the six Partitas (Clavierübung part I), the Goldberg Variations (Clavierübung part IV), the fifteen Two-Part Inventions and the fifteen Three-Part Sinfonias. Clearly reproduced on large sheets with ample margins; eminently playable. vi + 312pp. 8⅛ x 11. 22360-4 Paperbound $5.00

THE MUSIC OF BACH: AN INTRODUCTION, Charles Sanford Terry. A fine, nontechnical introduction to Bach's music, both instrumental and vocal. Covers organ music, chamber music, passion music, other types. Analyzes themes, developments, innovations. x + 114pp. 21075-8 Paperbound $1.25

BEETHOVEN AND HIS NINE SYMPHONIES, Sir George Grove. Noted British musicologist provides best history, analysis, commentary on symphonies. Very thorough, rigorously accurate; necessary to both advanced student and amateur music lover. 436 musical passages. vii + 407 pp. 20334-4 Paperbound $2.50

JOHANN SEBASTIAN BACH, Philipp Spitta. One of the great classics of musicology, this definitive analysis of Bach's music (and life) has never been surpassed. Lucid, nontechnical analyses of hundreds of pieces (30 pages devoted to St. Matthew Passion, 26 to B Minor Mass). Also includes major analysis of 18th-century music. 450 musical examples. 40-page musical supplement. Total of xx + 1799pp.

(EUK) 22278-0, 22279-9 Two volumes, Clothbound $15.00

MOZART AND HIS PIANO CONCERTOS, Cuthbert Girdlestone. The only full-length study of an important area of Mozart's creativity. Provides detailed analyses of all 23 concertos, traces inspirational sources. 417 musical examples. Second edition. 509pp. (USO) 21271-8 Paperbound $3.50

THE PERFECT WAGNERITE: A COMMENTARY ON THE NIBLUNG'S RING, George Bernard Shaw. Brilliant and still relevant criticism in remarkable essays on Wagner's Ring cycle, Shaw's ideas on political and social ideology behind the plots, role of Leitmotifs, vocal requisites, etc. Prefaces. xxi + 136pp.

21707-8 Paperbound $1.50

DON GIOVANNI, W. A. Mozart. Complete libretto, modern English translation; biographies of composer and librettist; accounts of early performances and critical reaction. Lavishly illustrated. All the material you need to understand and appreciate this great work. Dover Opera Guide and Libretto Series; translated and introduced by Ellen Bleiler. 92 illustrations. 209pp.

21134-7 Paperbound $1.50

HIGH FIDELITY SYSTEMS: A LAYMAN'S GUIDE, Roy F. Allison. All the basic information you need for setting up your own audio system: high fidelity and stereo record players, tape records, F.M. Connections, adjusting tone arm, cartridge, checking needle alignment, positioning speakers, phasing speakers, adjusting hums, trouble-shooting, maintenance, and similar topics. Enlarged 1965 edition. More than 50 charts, diagrams, photos. iv + 91pp. 21514-8 Paperbound $1.25

REPRODUCTION OF SOUND, Edgar Villchur. Thorough coverage for laymen of high fidelity systems, reproducing systems in general, needles, amplifiers, preamps, loudspeakers, feedback, explaining physical background. "A rare talent for making technicalities vividly comprehensible," R. Darrell, *High Fidelity*. 69 figures. iv + 92pp. 21515-6 Paperbound $1.00

HEAR ME TALKIN' TO YA: THE STORY OF JAZZ AS TOLD BY THE MEN WHO MADE IT, Nat Shapiro and Nat Hentoff. Louis Armstrong, Fats Waller, Jo Jones, Clarence Williams, Billy Holiday, Duke Ellington, Jelly Roll Morton and dozens of other jazz greats tell how it was in Chicago's South Side, New Orleans, depression Harlem and the modern West Coast as jazz was born and grew. xvi + 429pp.

21726-4 Paperbound $2.50

FABLES OF AESOP, translated by Sir Roger L'Estrange. A reproduction of the very rare 1931 Paris edition; a selection of the most interesting fables, together with 50 imaginative drawings by Alexander Calder. v + 128pp. 6½x9¼.

21780-9 Paperbound $1.50

AGAINST THE GRAIN (A REBOURS), Joris K. Huysmans. Filled with weird images, evidences of a bizarre imagination, exotic experiments with hallucinatory drugs, rich tastes and smells and the diversions of its sybarite hero Duc Jean des Esseintes, this classic novel pushed 19th-century literary decadence to its limits. Full unabridged edition. Do not confuse this with abridged editions generally sold. Introduction by Havelock Ellis. xlix + 206pp. 22190-3 Paperbound $2.00

VARIORUM SHAKESPEARE: HAMLET. Edited by Horace H. Furness; a landmark of American scholarship. Exhaustive footnotes and appendices treat all doubtful words and phrases, as well as suggested critical emendations throughout the play's history. First volume contains editor's own text, collated with all Quartos and Folios. Second volume contains full first Quarto, translations of Shakespeare's sources (Belleforest, and Saxo Grammaticus), Der Bestrafte Brudermord, and many essays on critical and historical points of interest by major authorities of past and present. Includes details of staging and costuming over the years. By far the best edition available for serious students of Shakespeare. Total of xx + 905pp.
21004-9, 21005-7, 2 volumes, Paperbound $5.50

A LIFE OF WILLIAM SHAKESPEARE, Sir Sidney Lee. This is the standard life of Shakespeare, summarizing everything known about Shakespeare and his plays. Incredibly rich in material, broad in coverage, clear and judicious, it has served thousands as the best introduction to Shakespeare. 1931 edition. 9 plates. xxix + 792pp. (USO) 21967-4 Paperbound $3.75

MASTERS OF THE DRAMA, John Gassner. Most comprehensive history of the drama in print, covering every tradition from Greeks to modern Europe and America, including India, Far East, etc. Covers more than 800 dramatists, 2000 plays, with biographical material, plot summaries, theatre history, criticism, etc. "Best of its kind in English," New Republic. 77 illustrations. xxii + 890pp.
20100-7 Clothbound $8.50

THE EVOLUTION OF THE ENGLISH LANGUAGE, George McKnight. The growth of English, from the 14th century to the present. Unusual, non-technical account presents basic information in very interesting form: sound shifts, change in grammar and syntax, vocabulary growth, similar topics. Abundantly illustrated with quotations. Formerly Modern English in the Making. xii + 590pp.
21932-1 Paperbound $3.50

AN ETYMOLOGICAL DICTIONARY OF MODERN ENGLISH, Ernest Weekley. Fullest, richest work of its sort, by foremost British lexicographer. Detailed word histories, including many colloquial and archaic words; extensive quotations. Do not confuse this with the Concise Etymological Dictionary, which is much abridged. Total of xxvii + 830pp. 6½ x 9¼. 21873-2, 21874-0 Two volumes, Paperbound $6.00

FLATLAND: A ROMANCE OF MANY DIMENSIONS, E. A. Abbott. Classic of science-fiction explores ramifications of life in a two-dimensional world, and what happens when a three-dimensional being intrudes. Amusing reading, but also useful as introduction to thought about hyperspace. Introduction by Banesh Hoffmann. 16 illustrations. xx + 103pp. 20001-9 Paperbound $1.00

POEMS OF ANNE BRADSTREET, edited with an introduction by Robert Hutchinson. A new selection of poems by America's first poet and perhaps the first significant woman poet in the English language. 48 poems display her development in works of considerable variety—love poems, domestic poems, religious meditations, formal elegies, "quaternions," etc. Notes, bibliography. viii + 222pp.

22160-1 Paperbound $2.00

THREE GOTHIC NOVELS: THE CASTLE OF OTRANTO BY HORACE WALPOLE; VATHEK BY WILLIAM BECKFORD; THE VAMPYRE BY JOHN POLIDORI, WITH FRAGMENT OF A NOVEL BY LORD BYRON, edited by E. F. Bleiler. The first Gothic novel, by Walpole; the finest Oriental tale in English, by Beckford; powerful Romantic supernatural story in versions by Polidori and Byron. All extremely important in history of literature; all still exciting, packed with supernatural thrills, ghosts, haunted castles, magic, etc. xl + 291pp.

21232-7 Paperbound $2.00

THE BEST TALES OF HOFFMANN, E. T. A. Hoffmann. 10 of Hoffmann's most important stories, in modern re-editings of standard translations: Nutcracker and the King of Mice, Signor Formica, Automata, The Sandman, Rath Krespel, The Golden Flowerpot, Master Martin the Cooper, The Mines of Falun, The King's Betrothed, A New Year's Eve Adventure. 7 illustrations by Hoffmann. Edited by E. F. Bleiler. xxxix + 419pp.

21793-0 Paperbound $2.50

GHOST AND HORROR STORIES OF AMBROSE BIERCE, Ambrose Bierce. 23 strikingly modern stories of the horrors latent in the human mind: The Eyes of the Panther, The Damned Thing, An Occurrence at Owl Creek Bridge, An Inhabitant of Carcosa, etc., plus the dream-essay, Visions of the Night. Edited by E. F. Bleiler. xxii + 199pp.

20767-6 Paperbound $1.50

BEST GHOST STORIES OF J. S. LEFANU, J. Sheridan LeFanu. Finest stories by Victorian master often considered greatest supernatural writer of all. Carmilla, Green Tea, The Haunted Baronet, The Familiar, and 12 others. Most never before available in the U. S. A. Edited by E. F. Bleiler. 8 illustrations from Victorian publications. xvii + 467pp.

20415-4 Paperbound $3.00

THE TIME STREAM, THE GREATEST ADVENTURE, AND THE PURPLE SAPPHIRE— THREE SCIENCE FICTION NOVELS, John Taine (Eric Temple Bell). Great American mathematician was also foremost science fiction novelist of the 1920's. *The Time Stream*, one of all-time classics, uses concepts of circular time; *The Greatest Adventure*, incredibly ancient biological experiments from Antarctica threaten to escape; The *Purple Sapphire*, superscience, lost races in Central Tibet, survivors of the Great Race. 4 illustrations by Frank R. Paul. v + 532pp.

21180-0 Paperbound $3.00

SEVEN SCIENCE FICTION NOVELS, H. G. Wells. The standard collection of the great novels. Complete, unabridged. *First Men in the Moon, Island of Dr. Moreau, War of the Worlds, Food of the Gods, Invisible Man, Time Machine, In the Days of the Comet.* Not only science fiction fans, but every educated person owes it to himself to read these novels. 1015pp.

20264-X Clothbound $5.00

LAST AND FIRST MEN AND STAR MAKER, TWO SCIENCE FICTION NOVELS, Olaf Stapledon. Greatest future histories in science fiction. In the first, human intelligence is the "hero," through strange paths of evolution, interplanetary invasions, incredible technologies, near extinctions and reemergences. Star Maker describes the quest of a band of star rovers for intelligence itself, through time and space: weird inhuman civilizations, crustacean minds, symbiotic worlds, etc. Complete, unabridged. v + 438pp. 21962-3 Paperbound $2.50

THREE PROPHETIC NOVELS, H. G. WELLS. Stages of a consistently planned future for mankind. *When the Sleeper Wakes,* and *A Story of the Days to Come,* anticipate *Brave New World* and *1984,* in the 21st Century; *The Time Machine,* only complete version in print, shows farther future and the end of mankind. All show Wells's greatest gifts as storyteller and novelist. Edited by E. F. Bleiler. x + 335pp. (USO) 20605-X Paperbound $2.25

THE DEVIL'S DICTIONARY, Ambrose Bierce. America's own Oscar Wilde—Ambrose Bierce—offers his barbed iconoclastic wisdom in over 1,000 definitions hailed by H. L. Mencken as "some of the most gorgeous witticisms in the English language." 145pp. 20487-1 Paperbound $1.25

MAX AND MORITZ, Wilhelm Busch. Great children's classic, father of comic strip, of two bad boys, Max and Moritz. Also Ker and Plunk (Plisch und Plumm), Cat and Mouse, Deceitful Henry, Ice-Peter, The Boy and the Pipe, and five other pieces. Original German, with English translation. Edited by H. Arthur Klein; translations by various hands and H. Arthur Klein. vi + 216pp.
20181-3 Paperbound $1.50

PIGS IS PIGS AND OTHER FAVORITES, Ellis Parker Butler. The title story is one of the best humor short stories, as Mike Flannery obfuscates biology and English. Also included, That Pup of Murchison's, The Great American Pie Company, and Perkins of Portland. 14 illustrations. v + 109pp. 21532-6 Paperbound $1.00

THE PETERKIN PAPERS, Lucretia P. Hale. It takes genius to be as stupidly mad as the Peterkins, as they decide to become wise, celebrate the "Fourth," keep a cow, and otherwise strain the resources of the Lady from Philadelphia. Basic book of .American humor. 153 illustrations. 219pp. 20794-3 Paperbound $1.50

PERRAULT'S FAIRY TALES, translated by A. E. Johnson and S. R. Littlewood, with 34 full-page illustrations by Gustave Doré. All the original Perrault stories—Cinderella, Sleeping Beauty, Bluebeard, Little Red Riding Hood, Puss in Boots, Tom Thumb, etc.—with their witty verse morals and the magnificent illustrations of Doré. One of the five or six great books of European fairy tales. viii + 117pp. 8⅛ x 11. 22311-6 Paperbound $2.00

OLD HUNGARIAN FAIRY TALES, Baroness Orczy. Favorites translated and adapted by author of the *Scarlet Pimpernel.* Eight fairy tales include "The Suitors of Princess Fire-Fly," "The Twin Hunchbacks," "Mr. Cuttlefish's Love Story," and "The Enchanted Cat." This little volume of magic and adventure will captivate children as it has for generations. 90 drawings by Montagu Barstow. 96pp.
(USO) 22293-4 Paperbound $1.95

THE RED FAIRY BOOK, Andrew Lang. Lang's color fairy books have long been children's favorites. This volume includes Rapunzel, Jack and the Bean-stalk and 35 other stories, familiar and unfamiliar. 4 plates, 93 illustrations x + 367pp.

21673-X Paperbound $2.00

THE BLUE FAIRY BOOK, Andrew Lang. Lang's tales come from all countries and all times. Here are 37 tales from Grimm, the Arabian Nights, Greek Mythology, and other fascinating sources. 8 plates, 130 illustrations. xi + 390pp.

21437-0 Paperbound $1.95

HOUSEHOLD STORIES BY THE BROTHERS GRIMM. Classic English-language edition of the well-known tales — Rumpelstiltskin, Snow White, Hansel and Gretel, The Twelve Brothers, Faithful John, Rapunzel, Tom Thumb (52 stories in all). Translated into simple, straightforward English by Lucy Crane. Ornamented with head-pieces, vignettes, elaborate decorative initials and a dozen full-page illustrations by Walter Crane. x + 269pp.

21080-4 Paperbound $2.00

THE MERRY ADVENTURES OF ROBIN HOOD, Howard Pyle. The finest modern versions of the traditional ballads and tales about the great English outlaw. Howard Pyle's complete prose version, with every word, every illustration of the first edition. Do not confuse this facsimile of the original (1883) with modern editions that change text or illustrations. 23 plates plus many page decorations. xxii + 296pp.

22043-5 Paperbound $2.50

THE STORY OF KING ARTHUR AND HIS KNIGHTS, Howard Pyle. The finest children's version of the life of King Arthur; brilliantly retold by Pyle, with 48 of his most imaginative illustrations. xviii + 313pp. 6⅛ x 9¼.

21445-1 Paperbound $2.50

THE WONDERFUL WIZARD OF OZ, L. Frank Baum. America's finest children's book in facsimile of first edition with all Denslow illustrations in full color. The edition a child should have. Introduction by Martin Gardner. 23 color plates, scores of drawings. iv + 267pp. 20691-2 Paperbound $2.25

THE MARVELOUS LAND OF OZ, L. Frank Baum. The second Oz book, every bit as imaginative as the Wizard. The hero is a boy named Tip, but the Scarecrow and the Tin Woodman are back, as is the Oz magic. 16 color plates, 120 drawings by John R. Neill. 287pp. 20692-0 Paperbound $2.50

THE MAGICAL MONARCH OF MO, L. Frank Baum. Remarkable adventures in a land even stranger than Oz. The best of Baum's books not in the Oz series. 15 color plates and dozens of drawings by Frank Verbeck. xviii + 237pp.

21892-9 Paperbound $2.00

THE BAD CHILD'S BOOK OF BEASTS, MORE BEASTS FOR WORSE CHILDREN, A MORAL ALPHABET, Hilaire Belloc. Three complete humor classics in one volume. Be kind to the frog, and do not call him names . . . and 28 other whimsical animals. Familiar favorites and some not so well known. Illustrated by Basil Blackwell. 156pp. (USO) 20749-8 Paperbound $1.25

EAST O' THE SUN AND WEST O' THE MOON, George W. Dasent. Considered the best of all translations of these Norwegian folk tales, this collection has been enjoyed by generations of children (and folklorists too). Includes True and Untrue, Why the Sea is Salt, East O' the Sun and West O' the Moon, Why the Bear is Stumpy-Tailed, Boots and the Troll, The Cock and the Hen, Rich Peter the Pedlar, and 52 more. The only edition with all 59 tales. 77 illustrations by Erik Werenskiold and Theodor Kittelsen. xv + 418pp. 22521-6 Paperbound $3.00

GOOPS AND HOW TO BE THEM, Gelett Burgess. Classic of tongue-in-cheek humor, masquerading as etiquette book. 87 verses, twice as many cartoons, show mischievous Goops as they demonstrate to children virtues of table manners, neatness, courtesy, etc. Favorite for generations. viii + 88pp. 6½ x 9¼. 22233-0 Paperbound $1.25

ALICE'S ADVENTURES UNDER GROUND, Lewis Carroll. The first version, quite different from the final *Alice in Wonderland*, printed out by Carroll himself with his own illustrations. Complete facsimile of the "million dollar" manuscript Carroll gave to Alice Liddell in 1864. Introduction by Martin Gardner. viii + 96pp. Title and dedication pages in color. 21482-6 Paperbound $1.25

THE BROWNIES, THEIR BOOK, Palmer Cox. Small as mice, cunning as foxes, exuberant and full of mischief, the Brownies go to the zoo, toy shop, seashore, circus, etc., in 24 verse adventures and 266 illustrations. Long a favorite, since their first appearance in St. Nicholas Magazine. xi + 144pp. 6⅝ x 9¼. 21265-3 Paperbound $1.75

SONGS OF CHILDHOOD, Walter De La Mare. Published (under the pseudonym Walter Ramal) when De La Mare was only 29, this charming collection has long been a favorite children's book. A facsimile of the first edition in paper, the 47 poems capture the simplicity of the nursery rhyme and the ballad, including such lyrics as I Met Eve, Tartary, The Silver Penny. vii + 106pp. 21972-0 Paperbound $1.25

THE COMPLETE NONSENSE OF EDWARD LEAR, Edward Lear. The finest 19th-century humorist-cartoonist in full: all nonsense limericks, zany alphabets, Owl and Pussycat, songs, nonsense botany, and more than 500 illustrations by Lear himself. Edited by Holbrook Jackson. xxix + 287pp. (USO) 20167-8 Paperbound $2.00

BILLY WHISKERS: THE AUTOBIOGRAPHY OF A GOAT, Frances Trego Montgomery. A favorite of children since the early 20th century, here are the escapades of that rambunctious, irresistible and mischievous goat—Billy Whiskers. Much in the spirit of *Peck's Bad Boy,* this is a book that children never tire of reading or hearing. All the original familiar illustrations by W. H. Fry are included: 6 color plates, 18 black and white drawings. 159pp. 22345-0 Paperbound $2.00

MOTHER GOOSE MELODIES. Faithful republication of the fabulously rare Munroe and Francis "copyright 1833" Boston edition—the most important Mother Goose collection, usually referred to as the "original." Familiar rhymes plus many rare ones, with wonderful old woodcut illustrations. Edited by E. F. Bleiler. 128pp. 4½ x 6⅜. 22577-1 Paperbound $1.25

TWO LITTLE SAVAGES; BEING THE ADVENTURES OF TWO BOYS WHO LIVED AS INDIANS AND WHAT THEY LEARNED, Ernest Thompson Seton. Great classic of nature and boyhood provides a vast range of woodlore in most palatable form, a genuinely entertaining story. Two farm boys build a teepee in woods and live in it for a month, working out Indian solutions to living problems, star lore, birds and animals, plants, etc. 293 illustrations. vii + 286pp.

20985-7 Paperbound $2.50

PETER PIPER'S PRACTICAL PRINCIPLES OF PLAIN & PERFECT PRONUNCIATION. Alliterative jingles and tongue-twisters of surprising charm, that made their first appearance in America about 1830. Republished in full with the spirited woodcut illustrations from this earliest American edition. 32pp. 4½ x 6⅜.

22560-7 Paperbound $1.00

SCIENCE EXPERIMENTS AND AMUSEMENTS FOR CHILDREN, Charles Vivian. 73 easy experiments, requiring only materials found at home or easily available, such as candles, coins, steel wool, etc.; illustrate basic phenomena like vacuum, simple chemical reaction, etc. All safe. Modern, well-planned. Formerly *Science Games for Children*. 102 photos, numerous drawings. 96pp. 6⅛ x 9¼.

21856-2 Paperbound $1.25

AN INTRODUCTION TO CHESS MOVES AND TACTICS SIMPLY EXPLAINED, Leonard Barden. Informal intermediate introduction, quite strong in explaining reasons for moves. Covers basic material, tactics, important openings, traps, positional play in middle game, end game. Attempts to isolate patterns and recurrent configurations. Formerly *Chess*. 58 figures. 102pp. (USO) 21210-6 Paperbound $1.25

LASKER'S MANUAL OF CHESS, Dr. Emanuel Lasker. Lasker was not only one of the five great World Champions, he was also one of the ablest expositors, theorists, and analysts. In many ways, his Manual, permeated with his philosophy of battle, filled with keen insights, is one of the greatest works ever written on chess. Filled with analyzed games by the great players. A single-volume library that will profit almost any chess player, beginner or master. 308 diagrams. xli x 349pp.

20640-8 Paperbound $2.50

THE MASTER BOOK OF MATHEMATICAL RECREATIONS, Fred Schuh. In opinion of many the finest work ever prepared on mathematical puzzles, stunts, recreations; exhaustively thorough explanations of mathematics involved, analysis of effects, citation of puzzles and games. Mathematics involved is elementary. Translated by F. Göbel. 194 figures. xxiv + 430pp. 22134-2 Paperbound $3.00

MATHEMATICS, MAGIC AND MYSTERY, Martin Gardner. Puzzle editor for Scientific American explains mathematics behind various mystifying tricks: card tricks, stage "mind reading," coin and match tricks, counting out games, geometric dissections, etc. Probability sets, theory of numbers clearly explained. Also provides more than 400 tricks, guaranteed to work, that you can do. 135 illustrations. xii + 176pp.

20338-2 Paperbound $1.50

MATHEMATICAL PUZZLES FOR BEGINNERS AND ENTHUSIASTS, Geoffrey Mott-Smith. 189 puzzles from easy to difficult—involving arithmetic, logic, algebra, properties of digits, probability, etc.—for enjoyment and mental stimulus. Explanation of mathematical principles behind the puzzles. 135 illustrations. viii + 248pp.
20198-8 Paperbound $1.75

PAPER FOLDING FOR BEGINNERS, William D. Murray and Francis J. Rigney. Easiest book on the market, clearest instructions on making interesting, beautiful origami. Sail boats, cups, roosters, frogs that move legs, bonbon boxes, standing birds, etc. 40 projects; more than 275 diagrams and photographs. 94pp.
20713-7 Paperbound $1.00

TRICKS AND GAMES ON THE POOL TABLE, Fred Herrmann. 79 tricks and games—some solitaires, some for two or more players, some competitive games—to entertain you between formal games. Mystifying shots and throws, unusual caroms, tricks involving such props as cork, coins, a hat, etc. Formerly *Fun on the Pool Table*. 77 figures. 95pp.
21814-7 Paperbound $1.00

HAND SHADOWS TO BE THROWN UPON THE WALL: A SERIES OF NOVEL AND AMUSING FIGURES FORMED BY THE HAND, Henry Bursill. Delightful picturebook from great-grandfather's day shows how to make 18 different hand shadows: a bird that flies, duck that quacks, dog that wags his tail, camel, goose, deer, boy, turtle, etc. Only book of its sort. vi + 33pp. 6½ x 9¼. 21779-5 Paperbound $1.00

WHITTLING AND WOODCARVING, E. J. Tangerman. 18th printing of best book on market. "If you can cut a potato you can carve" toys and puzzles, chains, chessmen, caricatures, masks, frames, woodcut blocks, surface patterns, much more. Information on tools, woods, techniques. Also goes into serious wood sculpture from Middle Ages to present, East and West. 464 photos, figures. x + 293pp.
20965-2 Paperbound $2.00

HISTORY OF PHILOSOPHY, Julián Marias. Possibly the clearest, most easily followed, best planned, most useful one-volume history of philosophy on the market; neither skimpy nor overfull. Full details on system of every major philosopher and dozens of less important thinkers from pre-Socratics up to Existentialism and later. Strong on many European figures usually omitted. Has gone through dozens of editions in Europe. 1966 edition, translated by Stanley Appelbaum and Clarence Strowbridge. xviii + 505pp.
21739-6 Paperbound $3.00

YOGA: A SCIENTIFIC EVALUATION, Kovoor T. Behanan. Scientific but non-technical study of physiological results of yoga exercises; done under auspices of Yale U. Relations to Indian thought, to psychoanalysis, etc. 16 photos. xxiii + 270pp.
20505-3 Paperbound $2.50

Prices subject to change without notice.
Available at your book dealer or write for free catalogue to Dept. GI, Dover Publications, Inc., 180 Varick St., N. Y., N. Y. 10014. Dover publishes more than 150 books each year on science, elementary and advanced mathematics, biology, music, art, literary history, social sciences and other areas.